Present Day English
for Foreign Students

BOOK TWO

Please ask the publishers for details of
PRESENT DAY ENGLISH:

Students' Books
Teacher's Books
Keys to the Exercises
Work Books
Graded Readers
Gramophone Records
Language Laboratory Exercises
Picture Books

Present Day English for Foreign Students

E. Frank Candlin, O.B.E., B.A. (Hons.)

Formerly Principal of the Oxford College of Further Education

BOOK 2

HODDER AND STOUGHTON
LONDON SYDNEY AUCKLAND TORONTO

ISBN 0 340 09016 2

First published 1962
Fifth edition 1968 © E. Frank Candlin
Tenth impression 1978

Illustrations by Bill Burnard

Printed in Great Britain for
Hodder and Stoughton Educational,
a division of Hodder and Stoughton Ltd,
Mill Road, Dunton Green, Sevenoaks, Kent
by Hazell Watson & Viney Ltd,
Aylesbury, Bucks

CONTENTS

PREFACE

THIS Course is designed for teachers who are looking for a class-book which will ease their task of lesson-planning and at the same time enable their students to make rapid progress in understanding, speaking, reading and writing everyday English.

The plan of Book Two follows closely on that of Book One. Each Lesson begins with a reading passage dealing with the daily lives of the Brown family and their friends. A piece of conversation follows, so that similar material is treated colloquially and more formally in the same lesson. Next come sentence-pattern drills illustrating points of grammar and usage, arranged to a carefully graded scheme, with explanatory notes added where necessary. The Lesson ends with a list of new words and idioms, and a plentiful collection of exercises based on the material of that and earlier Lessons.

To extend the 700-word vocabulary of Book One a further 600 words are here introduced, only about 40 of which are not in the *General Service List of English Words*. Phonetic transcripts are given for all new words and idioms as they occur in the Lessons, and again in the general vocabulary at the end. There is a reference index to the exercises, and a list of the sentence patterns showing the structure or teaching item covered in each. Once again the illustrations not only enliven the text but also provide further material for classroom exercises.

Teaching English as a foreign language is a highly skilled art, particularly when rapid results are looked for. It is hoped that this Course, based on much practical experience, will make the task easier for the teacher and the learning process more enjoyable for the student.   E. F. C.

KEY TO PHONETIC SYMBOLS

Vowels and Diphthongs

iː	siː	see, sea	θin	thin
i	siks	six	ðiːz	these
e	ten	ten	sed	said
a	bad	bad	pak	pack
aː	haːd	hard	faːst	fast
o	hot	hot	wot	what
oː	doː	door	koːt	caught
u	tuk	took	put	put
uː	buːt	boot	juː	you
ʌ	sʌn	son, sun	kʌt	cut
əː	səː	sir	fəːst	first
ə	'mʌðə	mother	'sistə	sister
ei	keim	came	eit	eight
ou	ʃou	show	nou	no, know
ai	lait	light	main	mine
au	kau	cow	raund	round
oi	toi	toy	boi	boy
iə	niə	near	hiə	here, hear
eə	peə	pear, pair	weə	where
uə	ʃuə	sure	juə	you're

Consonants

t	teik	take	put	put
d	dog	dog	had	had
p	pen	pen	map	map
b	buk	book	'teibl	table
k	'kofi	coffee	buk	book
g	gou	go	dog	dog

f	fɔɪ	four	haɪf	half
v	ˈveri	very	hav	have
m	ˈmʌðə	mother	kʌm	come
n	nain	nine	hand	hand
ŋ	siŋ	sing	ˈrʌniŋ	running
l	luk	look	dol	doll
θ	θin	thin	sauθ	south
ð	ðis	this	ˈfaɪðə	father
s	siks	six	buks	books
z	rouz	rose	dogz	dogs
ʃ	ʃal	shall	fiʃ	fish
ʒ	ˈpleʒə	pleasure	ˈviʒn	vision
tʃ	matʃ	match	ˈkwestʃn	question
dʒ	bridʒ	bridge	peidʒ	page
r	rʌn	run	təˈmorou	tomorrow
w	woɪl	wall	wen	when
j	jiə	year	jes	yes
h	hand	hand	hot	hot

LESSON 1

Wallpaper and Paint

Do you remember the Brown family, whom we met in Book One? There are four of them: John Brown, who is a bank manager, his wife Mary, and their two children, Susan, aged twenty, who works in an office, and David, aged eighteen, who is still at school. Then there is Susan's boy-friend, Tom Smith, who works in a factory.

As soon as the spring season comes round Mrs Brown decides that she needs new wallpaper in one of her rooms. This happens every year, and by now her family are used to it. This year it was the sitting-room. She saw that the paint on the doors and windows was dirty and that the curtains were old. When she told Mr Brown, at first he did not want to spend the money, but in the end he agreed. Mrs Brown usually gets her way!

Two days before the painter arrived, Mrs Brown moved out all the smaller furniture into another room and covered the rest of the furniture with large sheets as carefully as possible to keep off the dirt and dust. She took the pictures from the walls, washed the glass, and put them away in a cupboard. Then she took down the old curtains and rolled up the carpet. When everything was ready she sent for the painter.

The painter could not come the next day, so the Brown family could not use the room that day. The next morning the painter arrived just as they were having breakfast. His name was Stanley Nokes. First he cleaned off the old paper from the walls. Then he burned off the old paint from the doors and windows. Next he put two coats of paint on the doors and windows, and last of all he put the paper on the walls.

While he was working, Mrs Brown brought him a cup of tea once or twice, which he was glad to accept, but he went to a restaurant in the town for his dinner in the middle of the day. Mr Nokes is a quick, clean worker, and by the end of the second day the room looked very clean and bright.

The next day Mrs Brown hung the new curtains at the windows. They were of dark blue silk and they came down to the floor. When Mr Brown came home that evening she proudly showed him the finished room, and he agreed that he was as pleased as she was.

CONVERSATION

MRS BROWN (*at the breakfast table*): John.

MR BROWN (*looking up from his paper*): Yes, dear.

MRS BROWN: I was thinking . . .

MR BROWN (*putting down his paper*): Oh, dear! Tell me quickly—how much will it cost?

MRS BROWN: Don't you think we ought to paint and paper the sitting-room before the summer?

MR BROWN: It's not very dirty yet, is it?

MRS BROWN: Oh yes it is—it's as dirty as can be. And we want new curtains.

MR BROWN: But we did that room the year before last.

MRS BROWN: John, you know very well we did it three years ago. And we had those curtains when we came here, ten years ago.

MR BROWN: But we ought to paint the outside of the house this year, oughtn't we?

MRS BROWN: No. That can wait until next year. But we must do the sitting-room. I don't like to bring people here when the room is so dirty. May I ask Nokes to do it?

MR BROWN: All right. All right. Telephone him this morning. He'll do it well, and as cheaply as possible. But only one room this time. What about the curtains?

MRS BROWN: I've seen some lovely dark blue silk in Oxford Street. We'll go up on Saturday morning and then you can see it.

MR BROWN: I don't like to go up to London on Saturday. I go every day of the week.

MRS BROWN: But I don't, dear. We can get the new tools you want for the garden at the same time. It may be a fine day on Sunday, and then you can do some gardening.

MR BROWN: Yes, and it may be fine on Saturday and rain on Sunday. All right, then. You usually get your way, don't you?

MRS BROWN: Of course, dear. Now you must go, or you'll be late for your train. I'll telephone Nokes this morning.

. . . .

(*Later that morning*)

MRS BROWN (*telephoning*): Is that Bishopton three four three four? Can I speak to Mr Nokes, please?

MR NOKES: Nokes speaking.

MRS BROWN: Oh, this is Mrs Brown, Oak Tree House, Felton Road, Bishopton. Are you very busy just now?

MR NOKES: We're always busy, Ma'am. What can I do for you?

MRS BROWN: Can you paper and paint my sitting-room for me?

MR NOKES: When do you want me to come, Mrs Brown?

MRS BROWN: Can you do it either this week or next week— or even the week after next?

MR NOKES: I'm busy at the moment, but I may finish by Saturday. If so, I'll start on Monday. Will you come into the shop to choose the paint and paper?

MRS BROWN: All right. I'll be in town tomorrow morning; I may come in then, if I have time.

. . . .

(*The next Monday*)

MRS BROWN: Hello, Mr Nokes. We're just having breakfast. I shan't be a minute. I've got the room all ready, so you can start at once. Have you brought the paper?

MR NOKES: No. Today I'll get the old paint and paper off. I shan't put the new paper on until tomorrow. I shall need half a gallon of paint, or perhaps three quarts.

MRS BROWN: I want my husband to see the paper before you put it on. He hasn't seen it yet.

MR NOKES: I'll send my boy to fetch some of the paper from the shop. He's going to get some tools he's forgotten. He forgot the tools three times last week. I'll tell him to go as quickly as he can, but he may be a few minutes.

MRS BROWN: Thank you. Then my husband can see the paper before he goes out. I've cleared the room for you, so you may start as soon as your boy comes back.

. . . .

(*The next day*)

MR NOKES: I've finished now, Ma'am. Will you come and look at it?

MRS BROWN: Certainly. Well, Mr Nokes, that looks very nice.

MR NOKES: Yes, Ma'am. It *is* a bit cleaner and brighter, isn't it? Do you like the paper now it's on?

MRS BROWN: Yes, very much. It'll look nice with the new blue curtains and cushions. I shall put the curtains up tomorrow.

MR NOKES: I've put the best paint on. And the paper is very good too. It'll last a long time.

MRS BROWN: Thank you very much. I'm very pleased with it. Will you send me the bill?

MR NOKES: Yes. We'll see to that. Good-afternoon Mrs. Brown. And thank you for the cups of tea—with plenty of sugar, too!

SENTENCE PATTERNS

1.   *May*

May has two meanings: *permission* and *possibility*.
Notice that in speech we usually use *can* for *may* when we mean
permission.

(a) *Permission* (let, allow)

You may go home now, boys.
You may have the car tomorrow, if you drive carefully.
You may come again tomorrow, if you like.
She may have those books, if she wants them.
You may pick as many flowers as you need.
In this country children may leave school at fifteen.

May I open the window, please?   Yes, certainly.
May I pour you another cup of tea?   Yes, please.
                                          No, thank you.

May we come in?   Yes, do.
May I have this book, please?
May Tom stay to dinner, Mother?
May I carry your bag for you?

(b) *Possibility* (It is possible that, perhaps)

There may be some eggs in the chicken-house this afternoon.
You may catch the train if you hurry.
You may find him at home.
It may rain tomorrow.
I may finish this work by Saturday.
We may be hungry before we get home.
The work may be easier than we expected.
He may be cleverer than he looks.
She may be nicer than she seems.
It may be later than you think.
You may be wrong.

2.   Comparatives—Adjectives and Adverbs

(a) Adjectives

His garden is as large as ours.
Her new hat is as pretty as the old one.
Her hair was as yellow as corn.
She is cleverer than her sister (is).
John is taller than I (am).
This box is not as heavy as that one.
Birmingham is not as big as London.
He is cleverer than we think he is.
My bag is heavier than yours.
The sun isn't as hot as (it was) yesterday.
Her hair is not as dark as her sister's.

(b) Adverbs

He works as carefully as possible.
He ran as quickly as he could.
I will speak to him as soon as he comes.
We have lived here longer than you (have).
He goes to the theatre oftener than I (do).
She works harder than we do.
He drives much faster than I do.
He doesn't go to the seaside as often as we do.
We haven't finished as quickly as we did yesterday.
Have they lived here longer than we have?

3.   Agent Nouns in *-er, -or*

He teaches.   He is a teacher.
He acts.   He is an actor.

*driver; bather; swimmer; buyer; beginner; helper; learner; listener;
painter; reader; runner; rider; speaker; seller; singer; writer;
card-player; bell-ringer; conductor; baker; farmer; manager; waiter.*

NEW WORDS

bather ('beiðə)
beginner (bi'ginə)
buyer ('baiə)
cushion ('kuʃn)
dust (dʌst)
furniture ('fəːnitʃə)
gallon ('galən)
learner ('ləːnə)
listener ('lisnə)
lorry ('lori)
painter ('peintə)
paper ('peipə)
quart (kwoːt)
reader ('riːdə)
rider ('raidə)
runner ('rʌnə)
season ('siːzən)
seller ('selə)
sheet (ʃiːt)
singer ('siŋə)
speaker ('spiːkə)
swimmer ('swimə)
tool (tuːl)
waiter ('weitə)
wallpaper ('woːlpeipə)
writer ('raitə)

accept, accepted (ək'sept, ək'septid)
allow, allowed (ə'lau, ə'laud)
burn, burned, burned (burnt) (bəːn, bəːnd, bəːnd(t))
choose, chose, chosen (tʃuːz, tʃouz, 'tʃouzn)
cover, covered ('kʌvə, 'kʌvəd)
decide, decided (di'said, di'saidid)
expect, expected (ik'spekt, ik'spektid)
fetch, fetched (fetʃ, fetʃt)
forget, forgot, forgotten (fə'get, fə'got, fə'gotn)
last, lasted (laːst, 'laːstid)
may, might (mei, mait)
need, needed (niːd, 'niːdid)
seem, seemed (siːm, siːmd)

carefully ('keəfli)
certainly ('səːtnli)
either ('aiðə)
even ('iːvn)
once (wʌns)
possible ('posibl)
times (taimz)
twice (twais)

Idioms

   to come round (tə 'kʌm 'raund)
   by now (bai 'nau)
   in the end (in ði 'end)
   she usually gets her way (ʃi 'juːʒuəli 'gets hə 'wei)
   to send for someone (tə 'send fə sʌmwʌn)
   a coat of paint (ə 'kout əv 'peint)
   last of all ('laɪst əv 'oɪl)
   oh dear! ('ou 'diə)
   as dirty as can be (əz 'dəɪti əz kən 'biɪ)
   I shan't be a minute (ai 'ʃaɪnt bi ə 'minit)
   the week after next (ðe 'wiɪk aɪftə 'nekst)

EXERCISES

A. *Answer these questions in sentences:*

    1. Why did Mrs Brown want to have new paint and wall-paper in her sitting-room?
    2. Why did she want new curtains?
    3. Where did Mrs Brown buy her new curtains?
    4. What did Mr Brown buy at the same time?
    5. What was the name of the painter who did Mrs Brown's sitting-room?
    6. What were the Brown family doing when the painter arrived?
    7. What did he do first when he came to the house?
    8. What did Mrs Brown bring him while he was working?
    9. What did the painter's boy forget when he came to Mrs Brown's house?
    10. What did Mrs Brown do when her husband came home that evening?

B. *Put the right word into these sentences:*

    1. They went home when they (*have, has, had*) finished their tea.

2. Can you (*came, come, comes*) to London on Monday?
3. She hasn't (*some, any*) books in her bag.
4. Have they (*some, any*) flowers in their garden?
5. (*Do, did, does*) he go to the seaside last Saturday?
6. David is (*played, playing, plays*) football this afternoon.
7. Are there (*some, any*) people in the room?
8. Outside in the street it was (*rained, rain, raining*).
9. Don't (*runs, running, run*) into the water when it is cold.
10. Bob is the (*tall, taller, tallest*) boy in his school.

C. *Use these phrases in sentences, one sentence for each:*

I can do with; get on with; a lot of; not far from; at the beginning of; on the way; just inside; at first; in the end; the year before last.

D. *Finish these sentences:*

1. When they arrived home . . .
2. . . . while they were having breakfast.
3. After you have finished your lunch . . .
4. Before he went to London . . .
5. . . . when the water is cold.
6. While she was on holiday last year . . .
7. After they left the theatre . . .
8. . . . while the sun is shining.
9. When we get to the seaside . . .
10. After the match . . .

E. *Write ten sentences about the Browns' house in Bishopton.*

F. *Finish these sentences with a question-tag:*

1. He goes to London every day, . . .?
2. He bought a new car last week, . . .?
3. He'll take Susan to the theatre this evening, . . .?
4. They were having breakfast when he arrived, . . .?
5. They live in Bishopton, . . .?
6. He ought to do his homework now, . . .?

7. We can't go to the seaside today, . . .?
8. He hasn't caught any fish, . . .?
9. You don't go to school on Saturday, . . .?
10. She won't go to town tomorrow, . . .?

G. *Put the right pronoun into these sentences:*

  1. I gave the book to (*he, him*).
  2. We saw (*she, her*) in the garden.
  3. He met his friends and went with (*they, them*) to school.
  4. I saw (*he, him*) at the theatre, and he gave (*I, me*) some
     chocolates.
  5. This is the man to (*who, whom*) we sold the house.
  6. We met the man (*who, whom*) lives in the big house at
     the end of the street.
  7. Mr Brown saw his friend in the street and took (*he, him*)
     to the station.
  8. He spoke to me, but (*I, me*) did not answer.
  9. The sun was shining so (*we, us*) went to the seaside.
  10. Have (*they, them*) finished their work yet?

H. *Make these sentences negative:*

  1. You ought to do some homework today, David.
  2. Mr Brown caught some fish in the little stream.
  3. He found his friend in the garden.
  4. He'll have his lunch in school today.
  5. Tom went to town last Saturday.
  6. I'll finish this letter this evening.
  7. They're playing football this afternoon.
  8. Put those books on the table, David.
  9. He likes to swim when the sea is cold.
  10. We're going for a picnic tomorrow.

I. *Make these sentences plural:*

  1. His sister cooks very well.
  2. She hung a new curtain in the dining-room.
  3. I haven't a tree in my garden.

4. Does he know where the girl lives?
5. A child was swimming near the boat.
6. Have you a dog in your house?
7. This knife is mine.
8. Has he a box of matches in his pocket?
9. There was a loaf of bread on the table.
10. Is there a lorry in this street?

J. *Put the right preposition into these sentences:*
1. Mrs Brown was speaking . . . the painter.
2. The boy has left his tools . . . the shop.
3. Mr Brown went to London . . . his wife.
4. The Brown family are staying . . . home this evening.
5. Children must not run . . . a street in front of a car.
6. David jumped . . . the water.
7. The dog was asleep . . . the table.
8. Mrs Stansbury was looking . . . some eggs.
9. The taxi came . . . the corner.
10. The number six comes . . . five and seven.

K. *Make questions from these sentences:*
1. David has finished his homework.
2. She hung up the new curtains yesterday.
3. They took the bus to the station.
4. He likes to go fishing.
5. David went to school on Monday.
6. She is cutting the grass in the garden.
7. She arrives at the office at nine o'clock each morning.
8. They tear their clothes when they climb trees.
9. They have left their books on the table.
10. He swam to the little boat.

L. *Write a paragraph of ten or twelve sentences about the house in which you live.*

LESSON 2

David Has a Cold

ON Thursday of last week David came home from school in the middle of the morning. He said he was feeling ill; he had a headache, he was coughing and sneezing and every part of his body ached. David does not often have a cold, but when he does, it is usually a bad one; so his mother sent him to bed as soon as he came home.

That night he became worse. Mrs Brown was worried, and in the morning she sent for the doctor. Dr Cuthbert, the Browns' family doctor, arrived about a quarter to eleven.

Many people were ill and he was very busy. All the same, he took great care; he listened to David's breathing, looked at his tongue, took his temperature and asked how he was feeling. He said that David would have to stay in bed for a few days. Then he wrote on a piece of paper and told Mrs Brown that she must get the medicine at the chemist's at once. He shut his black bag, said "Good morning" and walked quickly out of the house.

When David is better, Dr Cuthbert will not send a bill to Mr Brown. In Britain everyone has to pay money each week from his or her earnings to the National Health Service. Then people do not pay any money when they have to go to the doctor or into a hospital. They pay a little for medicine, for new teeth and for glasses, but not very much. British people are proud of their National Health Service.

CONVERSATION

MRS BROWN: What's the matter, David? Why have you come home in the middle of the morning?

DAVID: I don't feel well. I was shivering and sneezing at school, and I feel very hot. Mr Clarke sent me home.

MRS BROWN: I think you've got a bad cold. A lot of people have got them just now. You'd better go to bed at once. I'll put a hot water bottle in your bed. Get undressed and jump into bed. Then I'll bring you some hot milk.

DAVID: All right, Mother. I think I shall be better in bed.

* * * *

(*The next day*)

MRS BROWN: Good morning, Doctor. I'm glad you've come.

DR CUTHBERT: Now, Mrs Brown. What's the matter?

MRS BROWN: It's David. He's got a cold, but rather a bad one, I think. He came home from school yesterday morning. He was hot and shivering, so I sent him to bed. He was very ill in the night, but he's a little better this morning. He doesn't often have a cold, but when he does, it's usually a bad one.

DR CUTHBERT: Well, let's go and see him.

MRS BROWN: This way, Doctor. David, here's Dr Cuthbert.

DR CUTHBERT: Now, David my boy. A cold, is it? There are a lot of them about. How are you—still alive?

DAVID: Well, I'm not dead yet, Doctor. I feel much better this morning, thank you. I'm not so hot and shivering now. Yesterday I felt very ill.

DR CUTHBERT: Good. Let me look at your tongue. Now your temperature. H'm. Not too bad. You've got a cold, but not a very bad one. You'll be well again in a day or two. Get this medicine for him, Mrs Brown, and give it to him three times a day after meals. Give him plenty to drink, but he'll have to stay in bed.

DAVID: When can I get up?

DR CUTHBERT: Not until I tell you. On Sunday perhaps.

DAVID: I want to play football on Saturday, Doctor.

DR CUTHBERT: Well, you can't play this Saturday, that's certain. Lie in bed, keep warm and take your medicine. I'll come in again on Saturday. Now I must go. There are hundreds of people in bed with colds in this bad weather, and everyone wants to see the doctor. Good-bye, David, I shall have to hurry.

DAVID: Good-bye, sir.

MRS BROWN: Thank you, Doctor. Good morning.

SENTENCE PATTERNS

4.   Indirect or Reported Statements

(a) When the *saying* verb is in the Present, Present Perfect or
Future Tense, the following verb does not change its tense,
but the pronoun usually changes to the third person.

He says he is feeling ill.—"I am feeling ill."
Mrs Brown says David can have an egg for breakfast.
He says he will come tomorrow.
They say they will visit us next week.
He says he was in London last Thursday.
Mrs Brown says she bought the oranges in town.

I think this is the cheapest coat.
He thinks he can finish his homework before tea.
I think we ought to go home now.
He thinks Susan is a very pretty girl.
I think Susan likes Tom.
He thinks he has lost his bicycle.

He knows she likes to go to the theatre.
I know David is a good footballer.
We know he has put the money in his pocket.

He tells me he has sold his house.
She tells me she is buying a new car.
They tell me they will have a holiday next week.

(b) When the *saying* verb is in the Past Tense, the following verb
is in the Past Tense. The pronoun usually changes to the
third person, unless the person reporting is *I*.

He said he went to London by train.
They said they were feeling ill.
Mrs Brown said Tom could stay to dinner.
He said he always went fishing in the summer.
He said he would come to see David on Saturday.

I thought I had the smartest hat.
We thought you were in London yesterday.
I thought he wanted a new car.
She thought there were some chocolates in the box.

He knew she was going to London.
We knew he liked fishing.
They knew we were going to the theatre.

They told the policeman they were waiting for a friend.
She told me she was going to Switzerland for a holiday.
Tom told me he was going to buy a new car.

5.   Indirect or Reported Questions

When the *asking* verb is in the Present Tense, the following verb does not change its tense.

When the *asking* verb is in the Past Tense, the following verb becomes Past.

In Reported Questions, the subject comes before the verb, as in reported statements: there is no inversion.

Where are you going?
becomes   He asked them where they were going.

She is asking him what he is doing.
He is asking them where they are going.
They are asking us when we shall come back.
He is asking them why they are leaving Bishopton.
I am asking him how old he is.
He is asking the policeman how far it is to Buckingham Palace.
They are asking us what the time is.
She is asking us who went to the theatre with us.

He asked them what they were doing.
She asked him where he was going.
They asked him when he could come.
He asked us why we were going to London.
She asked him how old he was.

They asked how far it was to Birmingham.
We asked them what the time was.
He asked me who was going with us on the picnic.

6.   *Have*

We use *have* as an auxiliary or helping verb in the Present Perfect
Tense. *I have finished my work.* We also use *have* in these ways:

(*a*) *Have* (Possessive)

> I have (got) a book in my hand.
> We have (got) a dog at home.
> David has (got) a cold today.
> I have (got) a present for you.
> I haven't (got) a pen.
> She hasn't (got) a father or mother.
> They haven't (got) a garden.
> I haven't (got) time to visit him today.
> Have you (got) a match, please?
> Has she (got) many friends?
> Have they (got) a nice house?
> Have you (got) your ticket?

(*b*) *Have* (Customary)

> I have an egg for my breakfast every day.
> We usually have our holiday in August.
> She always has tea in bed in the morning.
> She has a walk before dinner.
> I don't have sugar in my tea.
> David does not often have a cold.
> These people do not have a large breakfast.
> We don't have an English lesson every day.
> Do you have milk and sugar in your tea?
> Do you have much rain in your country?
> Does he have a holiday on Saturday?
> Does she have smart clothes?

(c) *Have* (Obligatory)

He has (got) to go to London on Monday.
She has (got) to catch a train at six o'clock.
They have (got) to stay at home today.
You will have to be careful.
They will have to leave at eight-thirty.
You don't have to do this if you don't want to.
He doesn't have to come every day.
They won't have to leave until tomorrow.
He won't have to work as hard as his brother did.
Will you have to buy a new car?
Does he have to go to London every day?
Do you have to finish this book today?
Shall I have to change trains at Crewe?
Shall we have to speak English all the time?

(d) *Have* (as Past Tense of *Must*)

Notice that *must* has no Past Tense. We use *had to.*

I must go home early.	I had to go home early.
We must finish our work before dinner.	We had to finish our work before dinner.
I must buy a new car.	I had to buy a new car.

Must becomes *had to* in Reported Speech.

"I must finish the exercise before I go to bed."	He said he had to finish the exercise before he went to bed.
"You must be more careful."	He said they had to be more careful.

NEW WORDS

body ('bodi)
bottle ('botl)
breathing ('briːðiŋ)
care (keə)
chemist ('kemist)
doctor ('doktə)

earnings ('əːniŋz)
glasses ('glɑːsiz)
headache ('hedeik)
hospital ('hospitl)
medicine ('medisin, 'medsin)

rather ('raːðə)

temperature ('tempritʃə)

tongue (tʌŋ)

tooth, teeth (tuːθ, tiːθ)

National Health Service ('naʃnəl 'helθ səːvis)

ache, ached (eik, eikt)

become, became (bi 'kʌm, bi 'keim)

breathe, breathed (briːð, briːðd)

cough, coughed (kof, koft)

could (kud)

earn, earned (əːn, əːnd)

feel, felt (fiːl, felt)

lie, lay, lain (lai, lei, lein)

shiver, shivered ('ʃivə, 'ʃivəd)

shut, shut (ʃʌt, ʃʌt)

sneeze, sneezed (sniːz, sniːzd)

undress, undressed (ʌn'dres, ʌn'drest)

worry, worried ('wʌri, 'wʌrid)

alive (ə'laiv)

bad (bad)

British ('britiʃ)

careful ('keəfl)

certain ('səːtn)

dead (ded)

great (greit)

worse (wəːs)

Idioms

on Thursday of last week (on 'θəːzdi əv 'laːst 'wiːk)

all the same ('oːl ðə 'seim)

he took great care (hi 'tuk 'greit 'keə)

he took his temperature (hi 'tuk hiz 'tempritʃə)

you'd better go to bed (juːd 'betə 'gou tə 'bed)

get undressed ('get ʌn'drest)

jump into bed ('dʒʌmp intə 'bed)

there are a lot of them about (ðər aːr ə 'lot əv ðəm ə'baut)

not too bad (not 'tuː 'bad)

EXERCISES

A. *Dictation:*

Bishopton is a pleasant little town about twenty miles from London. Many of the people who live there work in London and go up and down by train every day. In the High Street there are shops where people can buy food, clothes and things for the house. On Thursday, which is market day, the streets are full of people, cars and bicycles. Outside the town there are many large houses; the people who live here have plenty of money. The Browns have lived in Bishopton for ten years, and they like it very much.

B. *Answer these questions:*

1. Why did David come home from school early?
2. What did his mother tell him to do?
3. What did she bring him when he was in bed?
4. Why was the doctor very busy?
5. What was the doctor's name?
6. What did the doctor do when he came into David's bedroom?
7. What did the doctor give to Mrs Brown?
8. When can David get up again?
9. Why did David want to get up on Saturday?
10. Why won't the doctor send Mr Brown a bill?

C. *Write the words that the speaker used:*

He says he is going to London tomorrow.
"I am going to London tomorrow."

1. She says she likes going to the seaside.
2. He says he can swim well.
3. He is asking them what they are doing.
4. He said he was fishing all day yesterday.
5. He says he has lost his theatre ticket.
6. The policeman asked the driver why he was driving on the right of the street.
7. He says he goes to school by bus every day.
8. She said we could stay to dinner.
9. We asked them where they were going for their holiday.
10. She says it is market day in Bishopton today.

D. *Put* some *or* any *into these sentences:*

1. Have you . . . oranges in your basket?
2. She bought . . . bread and cakes at the baker's.

3. There were . . . small fish in the stream.
4. David hasn't . . . homework this evening.
5. Has she . . . money in her pocket?
6. We have asked . . . friends to come to tea today.
7. They haven't . . . flowers in their garden.
8. The teacher gave the boys . . . pens and . . . pencils.
9. Have they had . . . letters this morning?
10. We can't get . . . tickets for the football match.

E. *Put these words into sentences:*

hundred; suddenly; different; someone; building; while; easy; everyone; player; third.

F. *Put these verbs into sentences in the Present Perfect Tense:*

Do—He has done his homework.

go; find; think; put; see; come; take; make; run; send.

G. *Write ten sentences about any one of the Brown family.*

H. *Finish the second sentence:*
1. This is my book. This book is . . .
2. Those were their tickets. Those tickets were . . .
3. That is his pen. That pen is . . .
4. Where is your car? Where is . . .?
5. These are her flowers. These flowers are . . .
6. This is our house. This house is . . .
7. She has lost her ticket. She has lost . . .
8. Is that your car? Is that car . . .?
9. Are these my gloves? Are these gloves . . .?
10. Is that his coat? Is that coat . . .?

I. *Put the verbs in these sentences into the Present Perfect Tense:*
1. David is going to bed.
2. Mrs Brown will bring David some hot milk.
3. The teacher will send David home.
4. The doctor is taking David's temperature.

5. Mrs Brown is buying some fruit at the shop.
6. The doctor will write in his book.
7. The doctor will leave his bag on the chair.
8. Mrs Brown is putting a hot water bottle into David's bed.
9. Mr Brown will drive to the station by car.
10. The greengrocer will sell all his vegetables.

J. *Finish these sentences:*

1. Mr Brown says . . .
2. David thinks . . .
3. Susan wants . . .
4. Children like . . .
5. Mrs Brown said . . .
6. Her friend thought . . .
7. The teacher wanted . . .
8. Mrs Brown is asking David . . .
9. The policeman asked the children . . .
10. Mr Brown likes . . .

K. *Finish these sentences:*

1. David can't . . .
2. Susan must . . .
3. Tom ought . . .
4. Children mustn't . . .
5. Mr Brown oughtn't . . .
6. These boys can . . .
7. Can we . . .?
8. Must I . . .?
9. Ought you . . .?
10. David couldn't . . .

L. *Write ten sentences, using one of the following prepositions in each*:

over; under; between; near; on; with; across; beside; into; round.

M. *Rewrite the following sentences, putting a part of the verb* to have *instead of the verb in each sentence:*

1. Must I go to bed now?
2. I eat an egg for my breakfast every morning.
3. Is there a book in your bag?
4. He will go to Switzerland for his holiday this year.
5. You must be very careful.
6. Their garden is a nice one.
7. She always wears smart clothes.
8. Must they stay here all night?
9. There isn't time for me to visit him today.
10. It rained a lot during our holiday.

N. *Rewrite these sentences as reported statements or questions, beginning each with a verb in the Past Tense.*

1. "I'm not very well today."
2. "You must send for the doctor at once."
3. "Where is Susan going for her holiday next summer?"
4. "You can go now, if you like," said the teacher.
5. "How old is Susan?"
6. "I think I shall have a holiday on Saturday."
7. "I know where the Browns live."
8. "Who is Susan's boy-friend?"
9. "What are you having for lunch?"
10. "David isn't very ill," says the doctor.

LESSON 3

At the Chemist's

HERE is a picture of the inside of a chemist's shop. Mrs Brown is standing in front of the counter with a piece of paper in her hand. It is the paper the doctor gave her to get the medicine for David, who is in bed with a cold. The chemist is getting some soap from the shelves behind him for the other woman in the shop. Now he is ready to serve Mrs Brown. When she has asked for the medicine he will go into the little room on the right to put it into a bottle. He will then wrap the bottle in paper and give it to Mrs Brown. She will pay only twenty pence for the medicine, because in Britain people can have cheap medicine under the National Health Service. She is also going to buy a tooth-brush, a lip-stick, some face-powder for herself, and a comb and some razor-blades for Mr Brown, and some other things for the bathroom. She will pay the right price for these.

In Britain a chemist sells many things as well as medicines: soap, make-up, cameras and films, razors, shaving-cream, pens and writing-paper, and sometimes books. A chemist should always be very careful in his work; he must never give the wrong medicine or make a mistake by giving too much or too little. Doctors often write very badly and their writing is not easy to read. Chemists can usually read even the worst writing, but their work would be easier if the doctors wrote more clearly. Many years ago a chemist's shop was a very strange place, with strange medicines in brightly-coloured blue, green and purple bottles. Today you can sometimes see the big brightly-coloured bottles in the chemist's window, or on the shelves inside his shop (there are some in this picture), but now they fill these bottles with coloured water.

While Mrs Brown was waiting for David's medicine, her friend Joan Morton came into the shop. Mrs Morton asked how David was and Mrs Brown said he was much better. Mrs Morton asked what she could do to help. Mrs Brown said there was nothing she could do and everything was all right, but if she wanted anything she would telephone.

CONVERSATION

MRS BROWN: Hello, Joan. How are you?

MRS MORTON: All right, thank you. How's the family?

MRS BROWN: John and Susan are well, but David's in bed with a cold. He came home yesterday shivering and sneezing, so I called the doctor this morning. I'm getting some medicine for him now.

MRS MORTON: I'm sorry. Is there anything I can do for you?

MRS BROWN: No, nothing else, thank you. I can manage. I've finished my shopping, and when I get this medicine I shall go straight home. I don't want to leave David alone too long; he's by himself in the house.

CHEMIST: Now, Madam. What can I do for you?

MRS BROWN: Can you make up this medicine for me, please?

CHEMIST: Yes, Madam. Will you come back in about an hour? It will be ready then.

MRS BROWN: Would you mind making it up while I wait, please? I don't want to be away from home too long.

CHEMIST: Yes, certainly. Miss Harrison, make up this at once, please. (*To Mrs Brown*) Is there anything else I can get you, Madam?

MRS BROWN: Yes, there are one or two other things I should like: a tooth-brush, a lip-stick and some face-powder, please.

CHEMIST: Will you get those on the other side, please? The girl there will serve you.

MRS BROWN: This tooth-brush, please. And I want a lip-stick the same as this one. And some of this face-powder.

ASSISTANT: Very good, Madam. Is there anything else?

MRS BROWN: Can I get razor-blades at this counter?

ASSISTANT: Yes. How many would you like?

MRS BROWN: A dozen, please. Oh, and I want a man's pocket-comb. How much is that?

ASSISTANT: One pound and thirty pence, Madam. I'll put them in a bag for you.

CHEMIST: Here's the medicine, Madam. Is it for yourself?

MRS BROWN: No, it's for my son. How often should he take it?

CHEMIST: Three times a day, after meals. A cold, is it, with a high temperature?

MRS BROWN: Yes.

CHEMIST: This'll soon make him better. There are a lot of colds in Bishopton at the moment. This is the fifth bottle of this medicine that I have made up this morning.

MRS BROWN: How much, please?

CHEMIST: Only twenty pence. It comes under the National Health Service.

MRS BROWN: Oh yes, of course. (*To Mrs Morton*) Good-bye, Joan.

MRS MORTON: Good-bye. I hope David will soon be better.

MRS BROWN: I hope so, too.

MRS MORTON: Would you like me to drive you home?

MRS BROWN: No, thanks. John left me the car today, so I can drive myself home.

MRS MORTON: Will you be in town this afternoon?

MRS BROWN: No, I'm afraid not. I don't want to leave David. Now I must hurry. Good-bye.

SENTENCE PATTERNS

7.   Countable and Uncountable Nouns

Countable nouns take *a*, *an* with the singular form.
Uncountable nouns do not take *a*, *an*, and usually have no plural form.
Notice that we use *a* before a consonant, *an* before a vowel (*a, e, i, o, u*).

(*a*) Things you can count (Countable Nouns)

     a man, two men, some men.
     a book, three books, some books.
     an orange, four oranges, some oranges.

     Susan is going swimming with three friends.
     There are six chairs in this room.

There are some books on the table.
David tells the teacher that he hasn't a pen.
Mrs Brown hasn't any cakes for tea.
We haven't any flowers in our garden.
Is there a chemist's shop in the village?
Are there any letters for me today?

(b) Things you can't count (Uncountable Nouns)

bread, butter, milk, tea, sugar, coffee, meat, beef, cheese, water, food, grass, hay, corn, money, music.
He is eating bread and butter.
Grass is green and butter is yellow.
She gave him a glass of water.
Dogs eat meat and cows eat grass.
The farmer has some wheat ready to harvest.
The farmer gave some hay to his four horses.
Some music I like, some music I don't like.
He hasn't any money to buy food.
There isn't any grass in their garden.
I haven't any money in my pocket.
Do you like sugar in your tea?
Will you have some milk?
Will you have tea or coffee?
Have you any sugar in your coffee?
Is there any water in your glass?

8.   *Many; Much; A lot of*

(a) *Many*—with Countable Nouns

There are many men and women who do not like living in the country.
He has as many friends as I have.
Have they many flowers in their garden?
How many cups are there on the table?
We haven't many trees in our garden.
How many times have you seen her?

I have seen her many times.
There are many mistakes in this exercise.

(b) *Much*—with Uncountable Nouns

Do you have much rain in your country?
I don't think he has much money.
There is too much sugar in this tea.
She doesn't eat much meat.
How much milk is there in that bottle?
There isn't much difference between these two houses.

(c) *A Lot of*—with Countable and Uncountable nouns

Countable

He has a lot of trees in his garden.
They have a lot of children.
They brought a lot of dogs with them.
We've had a lot of rainy days this summer.
He grows a lot of vegetables in his garden.
There are a lot of mistakes in your exercise.
There were a lot of visitors at the National Gallery.

Uncountable

They get a lot of rain in Scotland.
We don't eat a lot of bread.
Doesn't he take a lot of sugar in his tea?
We do a lot of work in this factory.
There is a lot of money in this town.
There is a lot of butter on this bread.
There was a lot of chalk on his coat.
People don't drink a lot of wine in England.

Notice that in speech we use the shorter forms *much*, *many* in negative and interrogative sentences, but in affirmative sentences we usually use *a lot of*.

E.g. He had a lot of homework.
He didn't have much homework.

There are a lot of people here.
There aren't many people here.

9.   *Should—Would*

(*a*) *Should* = ought to

He should go to bed as he has a cold.
You should always be polite.
A chemist should be careful.
You should think before you speak.
People who live in glass houses should not throw stones.

(*b*) *Would*, would you mind = a request

Would you tell me the time, please?
Would you get me a paper, please?
Would you pass me that book?
Would you pass the sugar, please?
Would you type this letter, please, Miss Brown?
Would you mind if I shut the window?
Would you mind if we stopped here?
Would you mind if I had this chair?
Would you mind if we leave at once?
Would you mind if I have another cup of tea?

(*c*) *Should, would* in Indirect Statements and Questions after a verb of *saying* or *asking* in the Past Tense

We hoped that we should arrive in time.
I knew that I should be late.
We thought that we should catch the train.
He said that he would come again tomorrow.
He decided that he would go to London the next day.
They decided they would go to Switzerland for their holiday.

He hoped his friends would invite him for lunch.
She knew that the dinner would be ready.
John said that the home team would win.

(d) *Should, would like*

I should like to visit Wales.
We should like to go by air.
I should like to meet your sister.
We should like to read his new book.
He would like to learn to swim.
She would like to go shopping.
They would like to learn English.
Would you like to go home? Yes, I should.
Would he like to drive a car? Yes, he would.

Notice that in speech we shorten *would* and *should* to *'d.*

E.g. I should like = I'd like.
He would like = He'd like.

Many people now use *would* after *I* and *we* as well as after the other pronouns, except where *should* means *ought to*.

10. —*self* Pronouns

(a) *Reflexive*

He cut himself while he was shaving.
We lost ourselves in the wood.
They enjoyed themselves at the party.
We found ourselves in an empty house.
You should make yourself work harder.
You will hurt yourself if you're not careful.
I asked myself why I was there.

(b) *Intensive or Emphatic*

I did the work myself.
You must finish this yourself.
I don't want this myself; so you can have it.
I haven't a horse myself, but I enjoy riding.
I don't know her myself, but my friend knows her well.
The doctor himself did not know what was the matter with David.
We did not think the manager himself would show us round.

NEW WORDS

assistant (ˈəsistənt)
bathroom (ˈbaːθrum)
camera (ˈkamərə)
comb (koum)
difference (ˈdifrəns)
face-powder (ˈfeispaudə)
film (film)
lip-stick (ˈlipstik)
make-up (ˈmeikʌp)
mistake (misˈteik)
price (prais)
purple (ˈpəːpl)
razor (ˈreizə)
 razor-blade (ˈreizəbleid)
shaving-cream (ˈʃeiviŋ kriːm)
shelf (ʃelf)
soap (soup)
tooth-brush (ˈtuːθbrʌʃ)
writing-paper (ˈraitiŋ ˈpeipə)

fill, filled (fil, fild)
manage, managed (ˈmanidʒ, ˈmanidʒd)

pass, passed (pais, paist)
serve, served (səːv, səːvd)
shave, shaved (ʃeiv, ʃeivd)
should (ʃud)
would (wud)
wrap, wrapped (rap, rapt)

alone (əˈloun)
clearly (ˈkliəli)
high (hai)
nothing (ˈnʌθiŋ)
straight (streit)
strange (streindʒ)
worst (wəːst)

myself (maiˈself)
yourself (joːˈself, juəˈself)
himself (himˈself)
herself (həːˈself)
ourselves (auəˈselvz)
yourselves (joːˈselvz, juəˈselvz)
themselves (ðəmˈselvz)

Idioms

in bed with a cold (in 'bed wið ə 'kould)
to make a mistake (tə 'meik ə mis'teik)
everything is all right ('evriθiŋ iz 'ɔːl 'rait)
is there anything else? (iz ðeər 'eniθiŋ 'els)
he's by himself (hiːz 'bai him'self)
I can manage ('ai kən 'manidʒ)

EXERCISES

A. *Answer these questions:*

1. What did Mrs Brown buy in the chemist's shop?
2. Why is David in bed today?
3. Where will the chemist put the medicine?
4. How much did Mrs Brown pay for the medicine?
5. Why is medicine so cheap in Britain?
6. Name some things sold in a chemist's shop which Mrs Brown did not buy.
7. What is in the coloured bottles in a chemist's window?
8. Who was in the chemist's with Mrs Brown?
9. Why didn't Mrs Brown want to leave David too long?
10. How often must David take his medicine?

B. *Put the verbs in these sentences into the Present Continuous Tense or the Simple Present:*

1. He always (*come*) to see us on Thursday.
2. David often (*play*) football on Saturday.
3. Susan (*write*) a letter to her friend.
4. The children (*run*) across the sand.
5. Mr Brown (*like*) to dig in his garden.
6. He (*go*) to London every morning.
7. Susan (*read*) a book by the fire.
8. This evening David (*watch*) a television programme.
9. The birds (*sing*) loudly this morning.
10. Tom (*wait*) for Susan at the corner of the street.

C. *Finish these sentences with question-tags:*

   1. He isn't going to London tomorrow, . . .?
   2. He's in Birmingham today, . . .?
   3. She'll type these letters before she goes, . . .?
   4. He didn't play football on Saturday, . . .?
   5. We can't go to the seaside tomorrow, . . .?
   6. They are living in Bishopton now, . . .?
   7. They like going to the theatre, . . .?
   8. You haven't found your pen yet, . . .?
   9. Children mustn't run across the street, . . .?
  10. He ought to be in bed, . . .?

D. *Put a relative pronoun* (who, whom, whose, which *or* that)
    into these sentences (if necessary):

   1. We don't know the man . . . lives here.
   2. The boy . . . book is so dirty must do this work again.
   3. Have you seen the book . . . I left on this table?
   4. The policeman is looking for the man . . . left his car in
     the street.
   5. I gave him the book . . . I was reading.
   6. The woman . . . lives in that house at the end of the
     street is a friend of mine.
   7. The car . . . he is driving is not his.
   8. That is the man . . . we saw at the station yesterday.
   9. Those . . . have finished their work may go home.

E. *Put these words into sentences different from those in Sentence
    Pattern No. 7:*

   bread; music; money; food; tea; grass; water; meat; milk;
   cheese.

F. *Write questions to which these can be the answers:*

   1. I think so.
   2. We hope so.
   3. They said so.
   4. No, I don't think so.
   5. Yes, I'm afraid so.
   6. I hope not.
   7. I'm afraid not.
   8. We think so.
   9. They hope so.
   10. He hopes not.

G. *Put the right part of the verb into these sentences:*

   1. She has . . . a plate from the cupboard. (*take*)
   2. She . . . in an office in London. (*work*)
   3. They . . . to Switzerland for their holiday this year. (*go*)
   4. Tom was . . . in the sea. (*swim*)
   5. You can . . . across the road when the cars stop. (*run*)
   6. I have . . . my bag at the baker's. (*leave*)
   7. Susan is . . . until half past five this evening. (*work*)
   8. You ought . . . in bed today, David. (*stay*)
   9. Children must . . . their dinner every day. (*eat*)
   10. The baker has . . . the bread and cakes. (*bring*)

H. *Write the questions to which these are the answers:*

   1. While I was driving to the station this morning.
   2. Because she wanted some stamps.
   3. Because David was ill in bed.
   4. He is Susan's boy-friend.
   5. They live in Bishopton, near London.
   6. She is nineteen.
   7. They usually go to church.
   8. We bought them at the greengrocer's in Bishopton.
   9. Yes, I found it in the garden.
   10. They have one son and one daughter.

I. *Give a short answer to these questions:*

   Do you go to London on Saturday? No, I don't.
   1. Is Mrs Brown a good cook?
   2. Does David like playing football?

3. Can David get up today?
4. Ought children to run across the street in front of a car?
5. Did Tom buy a new car last week?
6. Will the sun shine every day next year?
7. Have the Browns sold their house in Bishopton?
8. Do Tom and Susan like going to the theatre?
9. Do doctors usually ride bicycles?
10. Has Mr Brown an orange tree in his garden?

J. *Put these sentences into the singular:*
  1. The boys have some books in their bags.
  2. Did these girls have any letters this morning?
  3. There are some tall trees in these gardens.
  4. Were there any chocolates in those boxes?
  5. Are there any pigs on these farms?
  6. We saw some pretty girls at the seaside.
  7. Do these boys play football on Saturday?
  8. The men have caught some fish.
  9. Shall we have some eggs for our tea?
  10. They don't know how old their friends are.

K. *Put the verbs in these sentences into two forms of the Future Tense:*
  1. We have bought a new house in Manchester.
  2. You went to the seaside with the Browns.
  3. The doctor visited David at his home.
  4. The doctor did not send a bill to Mr Brown.
  5. Did Mr Brown cut the grass in his garden?
  6. David is not doing his work well at school.
  7. They got home at twelve o'clock.
  8. When did you go to the theatre?
  9. The Bishopton football team won their match against Easthampton.
  10. I stayed in bed for three days.

L. *Write ten sentences about Dr Cuthbert. Do not take the sentences from this book.*

M. *Put the word* much *or* many *into these sentences:*
1. He said there was too . . . sugar in his tea.
2. How . . . does that pen cost?
3. Have they . . . rooms in their house?
4. Are there . . . boys in your class?
5. There isn't . . . milk in this bottle.
6. I have been to London . . . times.
7. You don't see . . . dogs in the streets of London.
8. Does she eat . . . meat?
9. You can have as . . . coffee as you like.
10. . . . hands make light work.

N. *Put the word* should *or* would *into these sentences:*
1. . . . you mind if I have another cup of tea?
2. I . . . buy a new car if I had the money.
3. He said that he . . . meet us at the station.
4. We . . . like to go to Ireland for our holiday.
5. . . . you like to see the garden?
6. Children . . . always be polite.
7. . . . you close the window, please?
8. We knew that we . . . be late.
9. They . . . live in London, if they could find a house.
10. You . . . look carefully before you cross the road.

A good soap
"Ten years ago I first used your soap.
Since then I have used no other."

LESSON 4

David Goes to Oxford

DAVID BROWN is now eighteen. He has been at the Bishopton Grammar School for seven years, since he was eleven. Now he is at the top of the school, studying English and Languages. He has worked hard during the past two years and the masters at the school think very well of him. Now, if he passes his examinations, he will go to a university where he will be a student for three or four years. He hopes to go to Oxford next October, at the beginning of the new term.

Last week David went to Oxford to take an entrance examination at one of the colleges, but he does not know yet whether he has passed. While he was in Oxford he was walking down the High Street, the most important street in Oxford, when he met a school-friend, whose name is Geoffrey Dixon. Geoffrey Dixon went to Oxford last year. He showed David all the interesting places and told him about life in college.

Oxford is a beautiful city on the River Thames about fifty-five miles from London. Most of the colleges are of grey stone; they have stood there for many centuries. There has been a university in Oxford since the thirteenth century. It began when some teachers, each with a few students, decided to live and work together in the same house. Other colleges followed, and little by little the great university we know today grew up. The oldest college, Merton, began in 1264; the newest college opened its doors for the first time only a few years ago. So the university is still growing. If David can get a place in one of the colleges, he will be pleased. There are one or two boys from Bishopton Grammar School already at Oxford, so he will find some friends there.

CONVERSATION

GEOFF: Hello, David. What are you doing in Oxford?

DAVID: I've been here since Tuesday. I came to take an entrance examination.

GEOFF: At which college?

DAVID: At Queen's.

GEOFF: That's a very good college. How did you get on?

DAVID: I don't know yet. We shan't hear until next week.

GEOFF: What are you going to read?

DAVID: Languages.

GEOFF: How long are you staying in Oxford now?

DAVID: I'm going home on Thursday.

GEOFF: Stay a day or two with me and I'll take you round the city, and show you something of Oxford.

DAVID: Thanks very much. That's very kind of you. I'd better telephone my home, then they'll know where I am.

GEOFF: All right. I'm just going to the library to do some work. I shall be free at half past four. I'll see you outside Queen's College. Then we'll go somewhere for tea. Have you seen much of Oxford yet?

DAVID: No, I've been too busy with the exam.

GEOFF: Good. Then after tea we can decide what we'll do first.

· · · · ·

DAVID (*telephoning*): Long distance, please. Bishopton five two four nine, please. Hello, Mother. David here.

MRS BROWN: How have you got on? Was the examination hard?

DAVID: Not very. I think I've done quite well. I hope so, but they haven't told us the result yet. We shan't hear until next week. Who do you think I met here?

MRS BROWN: I don't know. Someone from the school?

DAVID: Yes. Geoff Dixon. I haven't seen him for more than a year—since he left school. He wants me to stay with him for a day or two. He's going to take me round Oxford. Do you mind if I stay?

MRS BROWN: Of course you can stay. I hope you'll have a nice time. Have you got enough money?

DAVID: Yes, I think so. I've still got about five pounds, and I've got my post office book with me, if I need any more.

MRS BROWN: All right. Well, have a good time. I'll tell your father, when he comes home. He isn't in yet. Take care

of yourself, and give Geoff Dixon our good wishes.
Good-bye.

• • • •

GEOFF: Sorry I'm late. It's twenty to five. I couldn't get
away before now. How long have you been waiting?

DAVID: Only ten minutes. I've been here since half past four.

GEOFF: If you don't mind, I'll put these books in my rooms
before tea. . . . You'll enjoy Oxford. You'll make a lot
of friends here and meet a lot of interesting people.

DAVID: It'll seem strange after school. But I expect I'll soon
get to know people.

GEOFF: Yes, you'll find it very different from school. But
you'll have some friends already. There are four or five
men from Bishopton here already, so you needn't feel
lonely. You'll find college life interesting, too. Living
and working with a hundred or more people of your
own age but all with different ideas is very exciting.
But you need plenty of money if you're really going to
enjoy Oxford.

SENTENCE PATTERNS

11.   *Need*

(a) To require

You need a new suit.

Your coat needs cleaning.

Some people need more sleep than others.

Mrs Brown needs new curtains in her sitting-room.

My pen needs a new nib.

You will need some more money.

Do I need a new hat?

Doesn't he need this book today?

Do we need all these flowers?

Do they need any more food?
She doesn't need any help from us.

(b) Interrogative, instead of *Must*, hoping for a negative answer

Need I do this work again? (I hope not.)
Need I come if I don't want to?
Need he go to England to learn English?
Need I tell you this again?
Need we have all the windows open?
Need we wash our hands before lunch?

Notice that when *Need* is the negative or interrogative of *Must*, we form the negative and interrogative without *do*.

(c) Negative of *Must*

You need not go home yet. (You must go home now.)
He need not wear a coat today.
She needn't come if she doesn't want to.
We needn't hurry.
He needn't work so hard next year.
They needn't think I'm going to do all the work.
You needn't speak so loudly.

12.   *Still—Yet*

Still = unfinished time; *yet* = so far, until now.

Has he come home yet? No, he's still in Oxford.
Have you finished yet? No, I'm still working.
Have they found him yet? No, they're still looking for him.
Have you brought me that book yet? No, it's still in my room.
Is it four o'clock yet? No, it's still only half past three.
Has she bought a new hat yet? No, she's still wearing the old one.

Still comes before the verb, but after an auxiliary; *yet* may have the same position as *still*, but is more often placed at the end of the sentence.
I haven't been to Switzerland yet.
We haven't had tea yet.

She hasn't learnt to drive a car yet.
They haven't sold their house yet.
They haven't spent all their money yet.
Susan hasn't come home yet.
Has David gone to bed? Not yet.
Have you finished that game? No, not yet.

I still have five pounds in my pocket.
It was still raining when we left London.
I am still waiting for an answer to my question.
They are still on holiday in Ireland.
He still goes to London every day.
Is he still living in the same house?
Can she still read without glasses?
Is he still in hospital?

13.   Indirect Objects

In these sentences the verbs take two objects, a direct and an
indirect.

I am asking you a question.
She has brought me some flowers.
They have found us a new house.
Please get me some flowers from the garden.
He gave her a new handbag for Christmas.
Can you give me some money, please?
Will you show us the way to the station?
Please can you tell me the time?
Mr Thompson teaches the boys English.
I have written her a letter.
The teacher read the children an interesting story.
Bring me some flowers from the garden, please.
Hand me that parcel, please.
The boy gave his girl-friend some chocolates.
Will you pass me that plate of cakes, please?
Mr Brown promised David a gold watch if he passed his exami-
    nation.

14. Prepositions with Expressions of Time

They arrived (got) home *at* five o'clock.
The play started *at* half past seven.

It is warm *in* summer and cold *in* winter.
We always go for our holiday *in* August.

They don't go to school *on* Saturdays.
Christmas Day is *on* 25th December.

I have been to London twice *during* this week.
We had a lot of rain *during* the spring and summer.

I'm sure it will rain *before* morning.
He always takes a cold bath *before* breakfast.

In England most shops are closed *after* six o'clock.
Mrs Brown does not like to work in the house *after* midday.

She has been in this country *for* three months.
I haven't seen her *for* a week.

He has been in London *since* last Thursday.
I haven't seen him *since* last Monday.

You must be home *by* ten o'clock.
I think it will be fine *by* this afternoon.

The new theatre will be open *from* January 1st.
The store will close *from* December 24th *to* December 28th.

NEW WORDS

century ('sentʃəri)
college ('kolidʒ)
distance ('distəns)
entrance ('entrəns)
idea (ai'diə)
language ('laŋgwidʒ)

library ('laibrəri)
life (laif)
master ('maːstə)
nib (nib)
result (ri'zʌlt)
stone (stoun)
store (stoː)
student ('stjuːdnt)
term (təːm)
top (top)
university ('juni'vəːsiti)
wish (wiʃ)

order, ordered ('oːdə, 'oːdəd)
require, required (ri'kwaiə, ri'kwaiəd)
study, studied ('stʌdi, 'stʌdid)

exciting (iks'aiting)
free (friː)
lonely ('lounli)
quite (kwait)
thirteenth ('θəː'tiːnθ)
whether ('weðə)

follow, followed ('folou, 'foloud)

Idioms

to pass an examination (tə 'paːs ən ik'zamin'eiʃn)
how did you get on? ('hau did ju 'get 'on)
get to know people (get tə 'nou 'piːpl)
of your own age (əv juə 'oun 'eidʒ)
do you mind if . . . (dju 'maind if)
to have a nice time (tə hav ə 'nais 'taim)

EXERCISES

A. *Dictation*

Oxford is one of the most beautiful cities in England, and its university is the oldest in the country. Every year hundreds of young people come up to Oxford from school to spend three or four years at the university, and they never forget their time there.

People who come from other countries like to visit Oxford while they are in England, for it has many interesting buildings. If you go to Oxford, you will see the colleges, many with beautiful gardens, the old churches, and the crowds of people, cars and bicycles in the busy High Street, the most important street in Oxford. If you like, you can take a boat on the river in the sunshine. You will enjoy your visit to this old city very much.

B. *Answer these questions:*

1. How long has David been at Bishopton Grammar School?
2. Why did David go to Oxford?
3. Which is the most important street in Oxford?
4. Whom did David meet in Oxford?
5. How far is Oxford from London?
6. Which is the oldest college in Oxford?
7. Which college does David want to go to?
8. What is the Browns' telephone number?
9. How many boys from Bishopton will David meet at Oxford?
10. How old is David now?

C. *Finish these sentences:*

1. If you go to London, . . .
2. If he has lost his pen, . . .
3. If Susan is late at the office, . . .
4. If Mr Brown is not well, . . .
5. If David works hard, . . .
6. If the dinner is ready, . . .
7. If you go to town this afternoon, . . .
8. If Mr Brown catches small fish, . . .
9. If she sees a coat she likes, . . .
10. If we don't hurry, . . .

D. *Use these adjectives in sentences:*

happy, most interesting, more important, smaller, hottest, most beautiful, white, hungry, younger, ready.

E. *Make these sentences plural:*

1. There is a book on the table for him.
2. This flower is the most beautiful I have seen.
3. He has a box of matches in his hand.
4. Does he eat a cake for his tea?
5. Is he going to buy that book?
6. Does she like milk in her tea?
7. The book which he gave me last week was very interesting.
8. He said there was a knife on the table.
9. The bus leaves London at eight o'clock.

F. *Put the verbs in these sentences into the Present Perfect Tense:*

1. We are visiting our friends this evening.
2. Susan will bring some flowers for her mother.
3. Will you find me a book to read?
4. He is eating an apple.
5. They are going to London by train.
6. She is making a cake for tea.
7. He will cut the grass in the garden.
8. Which book are you reading?
9. He will smoke a cigarette before dinner.
10. She is singing to her friend.

G. *Put the right word into these sentences:*

1. Do you know . . . book this is?
2. Is this . . . hat I found in the garden?
3. Mrs Brown has two children; she is . . . mother.
4. That is your coat, and this coat is . . .
5. Susan, where are . . . gloves? Have you left . . . in the car?
6. The dog has eaten . . . dinner.
7. Susan has left . . . gloves in the car, but I have . . . in my pocket.
8. She goes out with her friends, and he goes out with . . .
9. Does she like sugar in . . . tea?
10. Do you know . . . lives in that big house?

H. *Use these verbs in sentences, putting the verbs in the imperative:*
work; bring; come; tell; take; put; eat; make; do; give.

I. *Put* a, an, some *or* any *into these sentences:*

1. I have ... egg for breakfast every morning.
2. Have you ... oranges in your basket?
3. She put ... book on the table.
4. They have ... beautiful flowers in their garden.
5. She hasn't ... brothers or sisters.
6. He picked ... apple from the tree.
7. There aren't ... plates on the table.
8. I haven't ... pen or ... pencil.
9. She put ... milk in the tea.
10. He hasn't ... money.

J. *Write ten sentences about a city or town that you know well.*

K. *Put in the words left out:*

1. David is ... to Oxford in October.
2. Mr Brown has ... some fish in the stream this morning.
3. ... swim in that water; it's very cold.
4. I haven't ... him since last week.
5. He ... a tree and ... his clothes.
6. You must ... the car carefully through the town.
7. Susan doesn't ... to be late at the office.
8. Mr Brown has ... to London by train today.
9. She has ... in England since last January.
10. They ... , but they didn't hear anything.

L. *Put the verbs in these sentences into the Present Continuous Tense:*

1. He was living in a big house hear London.
2. He sat on a chair in the garden.
3. She will write a letter to her friend.
4. They had supper and listened to the radio.

5. Mr Brown has worked in his garden.
6. Mrs Brown cooked the Sunday dinner.
7. She bought some fruit in the town.
8. The farmer will take his pigs to market.
9. She made a cake for their tea.
10. Will he play football this afternoon?

M. *Put the word* yet *or* still *into these sentences:*

1. Has Tom had his lunch . . .?
2. She hasn't learnt to speak English . . .
3. Are they . . . living in Manchester?
4. Has David gone to bed? Not . . .
5. Susan is . . . having her breakfast.
6. We . . . have time to catch the train.
7. Has she bought a new house . . .? No, she is . . . living in the old one.
8. We haven't started tea . . .
9. David . . . hasn't finished his homework.
10. Is Tom . . . her boy-friend?

N. *Put the right preposition into these sentences:*

1. He comes home every evening . . . six o'clock.
2. How many times did you see him . . . the first half of last year?
3. We always like a rest . . . lunch.
4. They are going to the seaside . . . Saturday.
5. People wear warm clothes . . . winter.
6. David has not been to school . . . last Monday.
7. He has gone to live in Switzerland . . . a year.
8. I don't think he will be home . . . evening.
9. If you don't want to be late you should be at the station . . . five-thirty.
10. He comes to London . . . August every year.

O. *Pick out the indirect object in these sentences:*

1. She has given John a present for Christmas.

2. We told him what we were going to do.
3. I will find you an interesting book to read.
4. They asked us a lot of questions.
5. Mary has brought me a present from London.
6. Get me my coat and hat, please.
7. He gave his friend twenty-five pence.
8. They showed us the beautiful flowers in their garden.
9. He taught the boys English.
10. He wrote his wife a most interesting letter.

P. *Put these sentences into reported speech with the* saying *or* asking *verb in the Past Tense:*

1. "I've finished my work."
2. "How far is it to London?"
3. "David isn't at all well," says Mrs Brown.
4. "Where do you live?"
5. "My wife is cooking the dinner."
6. "I'll call on Mr Brook when I get to Birmingham."
7. "Tom and Susan will go for a picnic if it is fine."
8. "What are you going to wear at the party, Susan?"
9. "It is past lunch-time, and I'm very hungry."
10. "Our friends are coming to tea on Sunday."

Q. *Write sentences with an indirect and direct object following these verbs. You may use any tense:*

bring; buy; cook; find; leave; make; order; paint; sell; send.

What to See in Oxford

An Oxford student was showing some friends round the University. "There's Balliol College," he said. "And there," pointing to a row of windows on the first floor, "are the windows of the Master of Balliol." He picked up a stone and threw it through one of the windows. A red, angry face looked out of the broken window. "And there," said the student proudly, "is the Master of Balliol himself."

Balliol ('beiliəl)

LESSON 5

A Visit to a Factory

TOM SMITH is an engineer. He works in a factory which makes bicycles. He has been at this factory for a year; before he came to the factory he was studying engineering at the University of London. He does his work well, and one day he is going to be the manager of a big factory—at least, he hopes so, and Susan hopes so too.

The factory is a long, low building between the road and the railway about five miles from Bishopton. It was built about ten years ago. There are a lot of people working in the factory, and many of them live in the nearby towns and villages, and travel to the factory every day. Some of them are brought to the factory each morning in buses, and are taken home again in the evening. It is always very noisy in the factory, but the workers soon get used to the noise.

A few weeks ago Tom took Susan to look round the factory. She was very interested. She saw the workers cutting the steel tubes and fitting them together. Then the bicycles were painted, and the wheels and saddles were put on. The saddles and bells and rubber tyres are not made in this factory; these are brought from other makers and are added before the bicycles are sent out to the shops. Bicycles from this factory are sent all over the world.

When lunch-time comes, most of the workers have their midday meal in the factory. There is a good restaurant (a factory restaurant is called a *canteen**) and there is often a concert while the workers are having their meal. Susan stayed for lunch in the canteen, and found that a very good meal was served.

Many people in Britain work in factories. They make engines, machines and tools, clothes, boots and shoes, cups and saucers, knives and forks, blankets and sheets, motor-cars, motor-cycles and aeroplanes, furniture and so on. These are sold to other countries to pay for the food, the wool, the cotton, the tobacco and other things which we cannot make or grow here.

CONVERSATION

(*Susan arrives at the factory and Tom meets her at the door*)

Tom: Hello, Susan. I'm glad you've come. Did you find the way all right?

* Canteen (kan'ti:n)

SUSAN: Yes: I got off the bus at the corner, and walked a hundred yards along the road to the factory. It looks very clean and bright from outside.

TOM: Yes. Factories are not usually dirty places these days. We do all we can to make the work pleasant. Come inside, and first of all we'll see the Manager, then we'll go round the factory.

SUSAN: Good. I've put on some shoes with low heels.

• • • •

TOM: Mr Carter. This is a friend of mine, Susan Brown. She wants to see the factory, so I'm going to take her round.

MR CARTER: Pleased to see you, Miss Brown. I hope you find it interesting. I can't take you round myself because an important customer is calling to see me this morning. But Tom's a good guide; he knows as much about the place as I do.

SUSAN: Thank you, Mr Carter. I'm sure I shall enjoy it. Tom has told me so much about the interesting things you do here.

MR CARTER: Good. There are a lot of things to see. I hope you'll stay to lunch with us, after you've looked round?

SUSAN: Yes, please. That will be very nice.

• • • •

TOM: Let's start at the beginning and see each part of the work until we come to the finished bicycle. In this store are the steel tubes from which the bicycle frames are made.

SUSAN: Do you make these tubes?

TOM: No. We buy them ready-made from a firm in Sheffield. The tubes are taken to this workshop and are carefully measured and then cut on these machines into lengths of one foot, one foot six inches, two feet, two feet six inches and so on—for the different parts of the frame and for frames of different sizes.

SUSAN: What do you do with the pieces when they have been cut?

TOM: They are joined together in this shop here. Then the wheels and chains and other parts will be added and at last we shall have a finished bicycle.

SUSAN: Are the bicycles painted here?

TOM: Yes. This is the painting shop. We don't use a paint brush. We use a machine. Watch that man over there. But mind you don't get the paint and oil on your coat.

SUSAN: How much does one of these bicycles cost?

TOM: Those there will cost about £20 in the shops.

SUSAN: Well, that was very interesting. How many bicycles do you make each week?

TOM: About five hundred. Half of these will be sold in Britain and half will be sold abroad. Now I expect you're tired of machines and ready for lunch. Let's go into the canteen; it's over there, next to the offices.

· · · ·

(At lunch in the canteen)

MR CARTER: Well, Miss Brown. What do you think of our factory?

SUSAN: Most interesting, Mr Carter. I'd no idea a bicycle factory was such an interesting place.

MR CARTER: Ah, that's because you had a good guide. And how do you like our canteen?

SUSAN: Very clean and bright. They serve a good meal here, too, don't they?

MR CARTER: Yes. People can't work well if they're not well fed.

SUSAN: Everyone looks happy here, Mr Carter.

MR CARTER: I'm glad you think so. I'm pleased to say there hasn't been any serious trouble here since I came eight years ago. By the way, did you come here by car?

SUSAN: No, I came by bus.

MR CARTER: We can't have that. Tom, you'd better run Miss Brown back to Bishopton in your car. But don't take the whole afternoon, will you?

TOM: Right. I'll be back as soon as I can. If you've finished, Susan. . . .

SUSAN: Yes, I'm ready. Thank you very much, Mr Carter. I've enjoyed my visit—and my lunch. Good-bye.

MR CARTER: Good-bye. I hope you'll come to see us again.

SENTENCE PATTERNS

15.   The Passive

We use the Passive in sentences where—if the sentence were active—the subject would be uncertain or impersonal or where the predicate of the sentence would be more important than the subject. The Passive is formed by the tenses of the verb 'to be' and the past participle. In the Passive, the subject of the sentence does not *do* anything (active); it has something *done to* it (passive).

(*a*) *Present*

The bicycle is painted green.
The wheel is fixed to the frame.
The factory is built near the railway.
Susan is invited to lunch in the canteen.
The workers are brought to the factory by bus.
They are taken home in the evening.
The tubes are fitted together.
The saddles and bells are put on.
The tyres are added to the wheels.

(b) *Past*

This bicycle was made in England.
The book was written in English.
I was given a ticket for the football match.
Our house was sold last week.
The food was well cooked.
Susan was invited to lunch in the canteen.
The tubes were cut into lengths of one foot.
The bicycles were sold in Britain.
They were taught English by an Englishman.

(c) *Future*

This bicycle will be sold abroad.
You will be invited to tea.
The furniture will be brought to your house in a van.
These books will be sold cheaply.
The boys will be sent to bed if they do this again.

(d) *Present Perfect*

The dog has been sent into the garden.
Susan has been invited to stay to lunch.
This car has been cleaned since last week.
The pigs have been taken to market.
The walls have been painted yellow.
All the windows in the house have been broken.

(e) *Past Continuous*

A house was being built for us at Bishopton.
Susan was being taught to swim.
She was being taken round the farm.
The rooms were being cleaned.
The boys were being taught English.
The baby was being washed and dressed.

P.E. II – 5

16.   Passive—Negative

(a) *Present Simple*

Football is not played in summer.
Bread is not sold by the greengrocer.
This box is not made of wood.
These flowers are not found in England.

(b) *Present Continuous*

Motor-cars are not being made in this factory.
This house is not being sold until next month.
This work is not being done well.
Long skirts are not being worn this summer.

(c) *Past*

That window was not broken yesterday.
This book was not written in England.
The boys were not allowed to play football yesterday.
David and his sister were not invited to the party.

(d) *Present Perfect*

This grass has not been cut this week.
The house has not been sold.
The car has not been put in the garage.
This dog has not been taught to look after sheep.
We have not been told what has happened.
The workers have not been taken home yet.

(e) *Past Continuous*

The books were not being sold.
The boys were not being taught well.
The children were not being helped with their homework.
The car was not being driven carefully.
The pigs were not being taken to market.

(f) *Future*

You will not be allowed to go home.
This shop will not be closed tomorrow.
Large hats will not be worn this summer.
We shall not be invited here again.
I shall not (shan't) be allowed to drive the new car.

17. Passive—Interrogative

(a) *Present Simple*

Is the wheel fixed to the frame?
Is the factory built near the railway?
Is the bicycle painted green?
Are the workers brought to the factory by bus?
Are oranges grown in England?

(b) *Present Continuous*

Is this boy being taught English?
Is your house being painted this spring?
Are bicycles being made in this factory?
Are long skirts being worn this summer?
Are these boys being given a holiday today?

(c) *Past*

Was that window broken yesterday?
Was this tree planted by the Queen?
Was the Tower of London built last year?
Were the boys allowed to play football yesterday?
Were David and his sister invited to the party?

(d) *Present Perfect*

Has the grass been cut this week?
Has the house been sold yet?
Has the car been put into the garage?
Have the workers been taken home by bus?

(e) Past Continuous

Was Susan being taught to swim?
Was the car being driven to the station?
Was a house being built for them at Bishopton?
Were the boys being taught English?

(f) Future

Will this shop be closed tomorrow?
Shall we be allowed to drive the new car?
Will you be invited to the party next week?
Will all the bicycles be sold abroad?
When will these curtains be taken down?

18.   *Let's* (= let us)

(*Let us* is the Imperative for the first person plural pronoun *We*.
    Let's is used instead of *shall we* to make a suggestion.)

Let's go to the seaside on Saturday.
Let's go by car, shall we?
Let's start at the beginning.
Let's look at the garden.
Let's go for a walk, shall we?
Let's have a cup of tea.
Let's see if your exercise is right.
Let's take the dog with us, shall we?

19.   *By* (Travel)

David goes to school by bus.
Mr Brown goes to the station by car.
Mr Brook goes to London by train.
We shall cross to Ireland by steamer.
My wife doesn't like to travel by air.
Some of the workers go to work by bicycle.
I am always ill if I travel by sea.

(But *on foot, on horseback*)
Some of the soldiers were on foot, some were on horseback.

NEW WORDS

aeroplane ('eərəplein)
blanket ('blaŋkit)
concert ('konsət)
cotton ('kotn)
engine ('endʒin)
   engineer ('endʒi'niə)
   engineering ('endʒi'niəriŋ)
frame (freim)
guide (gaid)
hedge (hedʒ)
heel (hiːl)
inch (intʃ)
length (leŋθ)
machine (mə'ʃiːn)
noise (noiz)
oil (oil)
part (paːt)
railway ('reilwei)
rubber ('rʌbə)
saddle ('sadl)
size (saiz)
steamer ('stiːmə)
steel (stiːl)
tobacco (tə'bakou)

trouble ('trʌbl)
tube (tjuːb)
tyre (taiə)
village ('vilidʒ)
workshop ('wəːkʃop)
world (wəːld)
yard (jaːd)

fit, fitted (fit, 'fitid)
fix, fixed (fiks, fikst)
measure, measured ('meʒə, 'meʒəd)
travel, travelled ('travl, 'travld)

abroad (ə'broːd)
bright (brait)
horseback ('hoːsbak)
kindly ('kaindli)
least (liːst)
low (lou)
nearby ('niə'bai)
noisy ('noizi)
serious ('siriəs)
uncertain (ʌn'səːtn)

Idioms

at least (ət 'liːst)
first of all ('fəːst əv 'oːl)
and so on (ənd 'sou on)
over there ('ouvə 'ðeə)
I'd no idea that (aid 'nou ai'diə ðət)
how do you like . . .? ('hau dju 'laik)
by the way ('bai ðə 'wei)
we can't have that (wi 'kaːnt hav 'ðat)

EXERCISES

A. *Answer these questions in sentences:*

1. How old are Susan and David Brown?
2. What is a factory?
3. Why does Susan hope that Tom will be a manager one day?
4. Where is Tom's factory?
5. How do the workers come to the factory each morning?
6. What is a canteen?
7. Why does Britain send bicycles and other things abroad?
8. Why does Britain buy food from other countries?
9. How are the bicycles painted?
10. How many bicycles does Tom's factory make each week?

B. *Write a composition about the Brown family, saying what you know about each person.*

C. *Put the right form of the Present Tense into these sentences:*

1. Every day Tom (*go*) to work in his factory.
2. Susan (*visit*) Tom's factory today.
3. She (*have*) lunch with the Manager.
4. Mr Brown (*drive*) to the station every morning.
5. Mr Brown (*walk*) to the station this morning.
6. The Manager (*think*) Tom is a clever young man.
7. The Browns (*live*) in Bishopton.
8. When Susan is at the office, she (*type*) letters for Mr Robinson.
9. David (*play*) football every Saturday.
10. Now the dog (*sit*) under my chair in the garden.

D. *Make these sentences negative (Use the shortened forms with* n't):

1. There are some bicycles in this factory.
2. Susan found her way to the factory.
3. The Brown family often go to the seaside on Saturday.

4. Mrs Brown cooked the dinner today.
5. Mr Brook walks to the station every day.
6. I had my tea at home yesterday.
7. She saw the bus leave the factory.
8. He is going to finish his homework before tea.
9. Susan can swim very well.
10. It will rain tomorrow.

E. *Make questions from these sentences:*

1. Susan went to the factory with Tom.
2. There were some cars outside the factory.
3. Tom drives his new car to work every day.
4. Susan works in an office.
5. David must try to pass his examinations.
6. They swam as far as the little boat.
7. They have finished their work and gone home.
8. David likes to play football.
9. The Manager spoke kindly to Susan.
10. There will be some nice cakes for tea.

F. *Rewrite these sentences in the passive:*

1. Buses take the workers home each evening.
2. They have put the saddles on the bicycles.
3. They don't make boys work very hard in school today.
4. You can see the river from our house.
5. They will send these bicycles abroad.
6. Smoke filled the room.
7. We have sent the children into the garden.
8. Someone has taken all the flowers from the garden.
9. A van will bring the bread to your house.
10. David wrote this letter.

G. *Change the verbs in these sentences into the Past Tense or the
Past Continuous Tense:*

1. David is writing to his friend in Switzerland.
2. Susan goes to the factory to see the Manager.

3. The buses take the workers home in the evenings.
4. Mrs Brown buys some oranges in the town.
5. Mr Brown is standing outside his house.
6. Mr Robinson puts the letters on Susan's desk.
7. She is sitting in the garden reading a book.
8. They catch the last train to Bishopton.
9. He keeps his car in our garage.

H. *Tell in your own words how a bicycle is made.*

I. *Use these words in sentences:*

some; any; much; many; three; a few; no; a lot of; a little; one (number).

J. *Use these idiomatic phrases in sentences:*

to get used to; a friend of mine; I'd no idea; by the way; looking forward to; during the morning; of his own age; do you mind if . . .?; at the top of; plenty of room.

K. *Put the right pronouns or possessive adjectives into these sentences:*

1. I saw Susan yesterday and gave . . . a present.
2. He has bought some flowers for . . . mother.
3. You may have this book because it is . . .
4. We have taken these hats, but are they really . . .?
5. She may have that letter, if it is . . .
6. I was speaking to the man . . . house we bought.
7. Do you know the woman . . . daughter works in Susan's office?
8. The boys have given . . . homework to the teacher.
9. We have lost . . . way in the wood.
10. You do your work, and I will do . . .

L. *Finish these sentences:*

1. The Manager will meet Susan in the canteen if . . .
2. He has a large breakfast if . . .

3. Tom will soon become a Manager if . . .
4. We shall play football on Saturday if . . .
5. He must drive fast if . . .
6. Buy some presents for me if . . .
7. Go home now, if . . .
8. I am going to buy a new car if . . .
9. He likes to go swimming if . . .
10. You'll break that window if . . .

M. *Put the right form of the adjective into each of these sentences:*

1. He has one of the . . . cars on the road. (*fast*)
2. This is the . . . book I have read for a long time. (*good*)
3. The work you are doing today is . . . than the work you did yesterday. (*easy*)
4. The actress on the stage was the . . . girl I have ever seen. (*beautiful*)
5. Which is the . . . book you have ever read? (*interesting*)
6. Susan often wears . . . hats than her mother. (*expensive*)
7. David and his friend are both . . . (*tall*)
8. He said this was the . . . day in his life. (*important*)
9. They have a . . . garden round their house. (*lovely*)
10. Mr Brown was . . . than his wife when David broke the window. (*angry*)

N. *Make these sentences negative:*

1. Cricket is played in the winter.
2. His work is being done carefully.
3. This bicycle was made in England.
4. Susan has been invited to the factory.
5. The children were being looked after.
6. These carpets will be cleaned this spring.
7. The cows are milked by the farmer's wife.
8. Our car was stopped by the police.
9. Vegetables are sold by the baker.
10. Our car has been cleaned this week.

O. *Make questions from these sentences:*

1. These flowers are found in England.
2. The carpets are being cleaned today.
3. David was told to go home.
4. All the clothes have been washed.
5. The house was being painted last week.
6. Susan will be invited to stay to lunch.
7. These bicycles were made at Tom's factory.
8. These boys are being allowed to go home early.
9. David has been sent to bed by the doctor.
10. These eggs were found near the hedge.

P. *Rewrite these sentences in the passive:*

1. They built the school just outside the town.
2. The doctor has given him some medicine.
3. Many people read this writer's books.
4. Mrs Higgins does the spring cleaning in our house.
5. A car will take her home after the party.
6. They gave the children presents from the Christmas tree.
7. These boys have done some good work today.
8. They have taken the pigs to the market.
9. A bus will take the workers home in the evening.
10. Someone has cooked this meal well.

Has She Really?

Every lady in this land
Has twenty nails on each hand
Five and twenty on hands and feet
All this is true without deceit.

Did He Really?

King Charles the First walked and talked
Half an hour after his head was cut off.

deceit (dəˈsiːt)
nail (neil)

LESSON 6

Mr Brown in Edinburgh

MR BROWN was in Edinburgh on business for his bank. He had caught a train from King's Cross Station in London at ten o'clock that morning and now he had arrived in Edinburgh. It was five o'clock in the evening. He had enjoyed a comfortable journey and had had a good lunch on the train. He had booked a room at the Queen's Hotel a few days before, so when he got out of the train at Waverley Station he took a taxi straight to the hotel.

When he got to the hotel he signed the book, the clerk told him the number of his room and the porter gave him his key. He went up to the third floor in the lift, and the lift-boy showed him to his room. It was a comfortable room with a good bed. That night Mr Brown slept well until the maid brought him some tea at seven-thirty next morning.

Mr Brown had not been to Edinburgh for many years, and he was looking forward to seeing the city again. So when he had finished breakfast he decided to go for a walk before keeping his first appointment at eleven o'clock.

He came out from his hotel into Princes Street, one of the widest and most beautiful streets in the world. It has fine shops on one side and gardens on the other, with Edinburgh Castle high on its Rock and Arthur's Seat beyond. The Scots are very proud of their capital city. As Mr Brown walked along, he remembered some of the exciting events that had happened here and some of the great men who had walked along these same streets—the things they had done, and the books they had written. He was surprised when he looked at his watch and saw that it was almost eleven.

His first appointment was with an old friend, Ian Macdonald, the manager of the Edinburgh branch of his bank. Mr Macdonald spent some time showing him round the city. During the three days he was there, Mr Brown saw most of the places of interest. He visited St Giles' Cathedral, and the royal palace which is called Holyroodhouse; he walked along the narrow streets of Old Edinburgh and up to the grey castle. He found, too, that Edinburgh does not live only in the past. New Edinburgh has modern houses and wide streets. His friend told him that every year in September a Music and Drama Festival is held, to which people come from all over the world; new plays can be seen and new music can be heard, and visitors can meet people from other countries and talk about the things that interest them.

When, at the end of his visit, he sat in the train which was carrying him south to London he made up his mind that he must come back soon to spend a holiday in this city in which the past comes so close to the present.

CONVERSATION

(John Brown calls at the branch of his bank in Edinburgh, and meets Ian Macdonald, the manager)

IAN MACDONALD: Hello, John. Nice to see you. Did you have a comfortable journey?

JOHN BROWN: Yes, thanks. I came up yesterday on the 10 a.m. from King's Cross.

IAN MACDONALD: Have you found a good hotel? Where are you staying?

JOHN BROWN: At the Queen's in Princes Street. I booked a few days ago so I had no trouble at all.

IAN MACDONALD: Good. That's one of the best in the city. How long are you staying?

JOHN BROWN: For three days.

IAN MACDONALD: Do you know Edinburgh at all?

JOHN BROWN: No. I haven't been here for many years. We see you in London more often than you see us here. I shall be busy in the mornings, but I think I'll spend the afternoons looking round Edinburgh.

IAN MACDONALD: I shan't be very busy this afternoon. If you like, I'll take the afternoon off, and show you round.

JOHN BROWN: Thanks very much. That'll be very pleasant.

IAN MACDONALD: Right. Meet me here at twelve-thirty for lunch.

• • • •

JOHN BROWN: Have you lived in Edinburgh all your life?

IAN MACDONALD: No. I was born in the Highlands, not far from Aberdeen. Have you been to the Highlands?

JOHN BROWN: No. We usually go abroad for our holidays— either to Spain or Italy.

IAN MACDONALD: That is sometimes a mistake. There are many beautiful parts of Britain that you should see.

You should certainly spend a holiday in the Highlands one year.

JOHN BROWN: But you get a lot of rain there, don't you?

IAN MACDONALD: Not so much as people think. We have more hours of sunshine in the summer than many other places in Britain. The mountains and lochs* are very beautiful in the late summer and early autumn. You should visit the Western Isles, too.

JOHN BROWN: That sounds a wonderful idea. I must tell my wife about it.

IAN MACDONALD: You should come up to the Edinburgh Festival next autumn and then spend a week or two touring the Highlands. You'll enjoy it.

· · · ·

(*At Waverley Station three days later*)

IAN MACDONALD: Well, John. This is the London train. It's *The Flying Scotsman*. It'll leave in five minutes, so I'll say good-bye.

JOHN BROWN: Good-bye, and thanks for everything. I had expected to spend a dull day or two in Edinburgh on business, but thanks to you I've had a pleasant little holiday.

IAN MACDONALD: I'm glad you came. My wife enjoyed meeting you, too. Now, don't forget; bring your wife up for a holiday next year and we'll take the car and show you Scotland thoroughly.

JOHN BROWN: We shall be very pleased. If the rest of Scotland is as interesting and beautiful as Edinburgh we shall certainly enjoy it.

(*The guard blows his whistle and* The Flying Scotsman *moves smoothly out of the station on its four hundred mile journey to London*)

* *loch* is the Scottish word for *lake*.

SENTENCE PATTERNS

20. Past Perfect

(*a*) This tense is used for an action or event already past and finished at some moment in the past.

We had worked all day, and now it was time to go home.
He had booked his room three days before.
He had arrived at ten o'clock the night before.
She had met a friend and gone shopping with her.
They had enjoyed their day at the seaside.
He didn't want a meal because he had had lunch on the train.
He had been in bed all the morning, but now he was getting up.
He had done what they had asked him to do.
He had finished his work before he went home.
It had already started to rain when we set off.
They went to the theatre after they had finished their meal.
She had not read any books by this writer.
The hotel was full, and he had not booked a room.
He hadn't been to Edinburgh for many years.
She hadn't finished dressing when her friend arrived.
They were hungry because they hadn't had any dinner.
They had not seen this actor before.
It was already April and he had not planted any potatoes.
We had just finished our work when the postman arrived.
Had she finished her work when you called?
Had you read the book that she took away?
Had you seen the house before he bought it?
Had you learnt all the words in Book One when you started Book Two ?
Had you heard this piece of music before it was played last night?
Had you visited Switzerland before, or was that your first visit?
Had you met him before the day he visited your home?

(b) Past Perfect in Reported Speech

The Past Perfect Tense is used in Reported Speech where the verb in Direct Speech was in the Perfect or Simple Past Tense.

He said he had finished his work.
She thought she had passed her examination.
David asked Tom if he had enjoyed the match.
Mrs Brown told the doctor that David had gone to bed.
We thought he had gone to Edinburgh.
Tom didn't think Susan had missed the train.
Did Mr Brown say he had bought a new car?
Did the doctor ask you if you had taken your medicine?
He said he had already sold his house.

21.   Tense after Time Conjunctions

The Present Tense or Present Perfect Tense is used after time conjunctions *when, while, before, until, as soon as,* even when a Future Tense is used in the main clause.

I shall meet him when he arrives in Edinburgh.
He will visit you when he comes to England.
They will find me here when they get home.
I shall stay with some friends while I am in Ireland.
We shall come home when we have spent all our money.

Learn your lessons before it is too late.
You must go home before the clock strikes midnight.
You have time for lunch before the train gets to London.
Tom mustn't leave until he has finished his work.
I shall stay at home until the rain stops.
Don't go away until I come back.
We will have tea as soon as my husband gets home.
I will write to you as soon as I have any news.
We will turn on the lights as soon as it is dark.
David will go to a university as soon as he has left school.

22.   *Great, Big, Large*

Great—important

This soldier was a great man.

There is a great difference between London and Edinburgh.

She is a great friend of mine.

He has made a great mistake.

Big—in size

They have a big house in the country.

You *are* a big boy.

He had a big book in his hand.

The English usually eat a big breakfast.

He bought her a big box of chocolates.

But *big* is sometimes used for *great* in everyday speech:

You've made a big mistake.

There's a big difference between the two brothers.

Large—in size, wide

They have a large garden round their house.

We shall need new curtains for these large windows.

They have a large farm near Bishopton.

People do not buy very large pictures today, because most houses
are too small.

23.   *Small, Little, Less, Few*

(*a*) *Small* and *little* are the opposites of *large* and *big*. There is
not much difference in meaning between *small* and *little* but
small is usually more formal.

I gave the letter to a small boy.

She is such a nice little girl.

The Browns live in a small town near London.

We like our little village very much.

You have made a small mistake in this exercise.
It was only a little mistake.

Where two opposites are given together, we say *large* and *small*, *big* and *little*.

Do you want a large or a small box of chocolates?
I asked for a small glass of wine, but he gave me a large one.
We have a big house in London and a little house in the country.
Big boys go out to play football; little boys stay at home to play in the garden.

(b) *Little* is used for quantity with uncountable nouns, as the opposite of *much* or a *lot of*.

There is very little milk in this coffee.
Mr Brown has little time for gardening.
Please may I have a little more sugar?
There is a little wine left in this bottle.
We should like a little bread with this soup.

(c) *Less* is the comparative form of *little*.

I have done very little work today and I did less yesterday.
He has little money and he will have less if he is not careful.
We had less rain today than (we had) yesterday.
We use less coal in England today than (we did) twenty years ago.
He told the children to make less noise. (That is, less than they were making.)

(d) *Few* is the opposite of *many* and is used not for quantity but for a number of things, with countable but not with uncountable nouns.

There are a few eggs in this basket.
I have visited Edinburgh a few times.

He was spending a few days in Scotland.
There are very few flowers in the garden in winter.
You will find few books in that house.

24.   *So ... Neither ... Nor ...*

To save repetition we use short phrases beginning with *so ...* (affirmative) and *neither ...* or *nor ...* (negative) as additions to statements made.

(a) *Affirmative*

Tom likes going to the theatre, and so do I.*
If you can have a holiday, then so can we.
Mary went to London yesterday, and so did John.
We shall have a holiday on Saturday, and so will you.
David had an egg for breakfast, and so did Tom.
He walks to work every morning, and so does his brother.
"I must go to bed early tonight." "And so must I."
"The Browns were at the theatre last night." "So were the Robinsons."
"You ought to be more polite." "And so ought you."
"David could talk when he was two." "So could Brian."

(b) *Negative*

John hasn't been to the cinema since Christmas, and neither have I.
They haven't a garden, and neither have we.
I don't like London in August, and neither does Mary.
"I don't like onions." "Nor do I".
"We can't come this evening." "Neither can Mary."
"I couldn't do that exercise." "Nor could I."
"David can't come to the party this evening." "Nor can Tom."

* Notice that there is inversion of subject and verb after *so*, *neither* and *nor*.

NEW WORDS

appointment (ə'pointmənt)
business ('biznis)
capital ('kapitl)
drama ('drɑːmə)
event (i'vent)
festival ('festəvəl)
hotel (hou'tel, ou'tel)
isles (ailz)
journey ('dʒəːni)
key (kiː)
lake (leik)
lift (lift)
maid (meid)
mountain ('mauntin)
rock (rok)

born (boːn)
fly, flew, flown (flai, fluː, floun)
miss, missed (mis, mist)
plant, planted (plɑːnt, 'plɑːntid)

sign, signed (sain, saind)
surprise, surprised (sə'praiz, sə'praizd)
sweep, swept (swiːp, swept)

almost ('oːlmoust)
beyond (bi'jond)
close (klous)
comfortable ('kʌmftəbl)
dull (dʌl)
less (les)
modern ('modən)
narrow ('narou)
neither ('naiðə)
nor (noː)
opposite ('opəzit)
several ('sevrəl)
smoothly ('smuːðli)
thoroughly ('θʌrəli)
touring ('tuəriŋ)
wonderful ('wʌndəful)

Idioms

on business (on 'biznis)
showed him to his room ('ʃoud him tu hiz 'rum)
to go for a walk (tə 'gou fər ə 'woːk)
to keep an appointment (tə 'kiːp ən ə'pointmənt)
to live in the past (tə' liv in ðə 'pɑːst)
to make up one's mind (tə 'meik ʌp wʌnz 'maind)
to get in on time (tə 'get 'in on 'taim)
to take the afternoon off (tə 'teik ði' aːftənuːn 'of)
that sounds a wonderful idea ('ðat 'saundz ə 'wʌndəful ai'diə)
thanks for everything ('θaŋks fər'evriθiŋ)

EXERCISES

A. *Put the verbs in these sentences into the Past Perfect Tense:*

1. They (*lose*) their way in the wood.
2. He (*visit*) all the interesting places in Edinburgh.
3. We (*buy*) all the food we needed.
4. He (*have*) his breakfast before he set off.
5. Mr Brown (*be*) to Edinburgh many years before.
6. She (*find*) what she was looking for.
7. They (*drive*) to the station before nine o'clock.
8. He (*come*) to school by bus.
9. His father (*give*) him plenty of money before he left.
10. She (*write*) several letters that morning.

B. *Put* should *or* ought *into these sentences:*

1. You . . . eat a good breakfast before you go to work.
2. Children . . . always look before they cross the road.
3. David . . . to go to bed if he is ill.
4. . . . we go home now?
5. You . . . to drive carefully in a crowded street.
6. Chimneys . . . always be swept at least once a year.
7. David . . . give his mother a present at Christmas.
8. This team . . . to win the Cup this year.
9. . . . you to be out of the house when you are ill?
10. Tom . . . not to talk loudly in the theatre.

C. *Put each of these words into a sentence:*

may; can; could; must; shall; should; would; will; get; does.

D. *Finish these sentences with a time clause:*

1. I shall go home as soon as . . .
2. Tom will stay in bed until . . .
3. I'll ask him to call on you when . . .
4. You cannot buy anything after . . .
5. Get your hat before . . .
6. You can start to spend your English money when . . .

    7. We shall go swimming as soon as . . .
    8. Mr Brown will wash his hands before . . .
    9. No one may leave the house until . . .
  10. Let's hurry home before . . .

E. *Write down the short form of these words, as used in conversation:*

    must not; shall not; will not; cannot; does not; you are; they have; it is; I am; is it not; we shall; you would; you had; they are; did not; I shall; she is; she will; they will; ought not.

F. *Add question-tags to these sentences:*

    1. She never goes to London in August . . .?
    2. I may have these apples . . .?
    3. He bought these books in Edinburgh . . .?
    4. You will be at the station by six o'clock . . .?
    5. We shan't stay here all day . . .?
    6. There are plenty of empty seats in the train . . .?
    7. He isn't a friend of yours . . .?
    8. We are going to have tea with Mrs Brown . . .?
    9. You wrote a letter to him last week . . .?
  10. They live in Bishopton . . .?

G. *Put the correct form of the adjective or adverb into these sentences:*

    1. David is the (*good*) boy in the school.
    2. I think Susan is (*pretty*) than Joan.
    3. Tom works (*hard*) than the other men.
    4. Glasgow is the (*large*) city in Scotland.
    5. This is the (*interesting*) book I have ever read.
    6. Some people think Scotland is (*beautiful*) than England.
    7. Girls usually speak (*quietly*) than boys.
    8. Mrs Brown usually drives (*carefully*) than her husband.
    9. We saw a very (*good*) play at the theatre.
  10. You should not drive (*fast*) through a town.

H. (a) *Answer these questions with phrases which begin with* Because . . .:

1. Why did Susan go home early?
2. Why did Mr Brown go to Edinburgh?
3. Why was he looking forward to seeing Edinburgh again?
4. Why did Tom buy a new car?
5. Why did Mrs Brown want new curtains?

(b) *Write the questions to which these could be the answers:*

1. Because they enjoy watching plays.
2. After they had finished their supper.
3. Until next Friday.
4. Eighteen last June.
5. Five pence in one pocket and ten pence in the other.

I. *Put these sentences into reported speech:*

1. "Some of the streets of Edinburgh are very wide."
2. "I read the newspaper every morning," he said.
3. "I don't know what you are talking about," he said.
4. "The train arrives at three o'clock," she said.
5. "I am reading a very interesting book," she said.
6. "I think Tom is a clever man."
7. "I know how much money he earns," she said.
8. "There are a lot of shops in this town," she said.
9. "We shall stay here until next Tuesday," he said.
10. "I think it's going to rain tomorrow."

J. *Turn these questions into indirect questions:*

1. "Where are you going tomorrow?" he asked.
2. "Has the postman come yet?" she asked.
3. "Have you been here before?" he asked.
4. "Who is going with you to the theatre?"
5. "How old are you, David?" Tom asked.
6. "What time is it?" she asked.
7. "Do you know how far it is to London?" the driver asked.

8. "Can we have some flowers from your garden?" he asked us.

9. "Have you ever seen the man before?" the policeman asked David.

10. "Will you be going to Birmingham on Sunday?" he asked Susan.

K. *Use these nouns in sentences:*

milk; money; flowers; rain; books; meat; children; sugar; tea; bottle; people; fire; cups; fruit; water; sea; boats; glass; chalk; pen.

L. *Complete these sentences:*

1. . . . since last Thursday.
2. . . . since last Friday.
3. . . . since you came to this country.
4. . . . since he was last in Edinburgh.
5. . . . since they came to Bishopton.
6. . . . since he left school.
7. . . . since last summer.
8. . . . since four o'clock.
9. . . . since she was ten years old.
10. . . . since this house was built.

M. *Put the word* small, little, few, *or* less *into these sentences:*

1. There is very . . . sugar in my tea.
2. We have had . . . sunshine than we had last year.
3. There are still a . . . people who have not gone home.
4. They have such a pretty . . . daughter.
5. Tom works in a . . . factory near Bishopton.
6. We are staying for a . . . days in Bishopton.
7. Mrs Brown has used . . . milk today than yesterday.
8. May I have a . . . more milk, please?
9. There was a large book and a . . . book on the table.
10. He earns . . . money than his brother.

N. *Write a description of the largest street of a town you know well.*

O. *Add to these sentences a phrase beginning with* so:

Tom likes sugar in his tea, and . . . (so do I)
1. Susan can swim very well, and . . .
2. Mrs Brown likes a tidy house, and . . .
3. If you can do this exercise . . .
4. Tom went to London yesterday, and . . .
5. You have some trees in your garden, and . . .

P. *Write a description of your own family having their first meal of the day.*

Two for the Price of One

People say that the Scots do not like to spend money, and that when they do spend money they like to get as much as they can for it. There are many stories about this. Here is one of them:

In the Royal Albert Hall—a large concert hall in London —there are a few seats where you can hear every sound twice because there is an echo. These seats are always taken by Scotsmen, who can then hear a concert twice for the price of one ticket.

echo ('ekou) hall (hoːl) sound (saund)

LESSON 7

Mrs Brown's Tea-party

On the first Thursday in every month Mrs Brown invites her friends to have tea with her. People used to call this an 'At Home', but this phrase is not used so much today. The house is made very clean and tidy, and fresh flowers are put in the rooms. Plenty of coal is put on the fire in cold weather, for everything must look its best. In the summer Mr Brown is asked to cut the grass and tidy the garden and Susan and David are told not to leave their things about. David says he can always tell when it is 'Mother's Thursday'; if he is at home he stays in his own room.

The guests arrive about three and soon the sitting-room is full of Mrs Brown's friends, all talking at once. They talk about their homes, their families, their friends, clothes, the cost of things in the shops; they tell each other about their holiday plans, the plays, films and television programmes they have seen, and sometimes the things that other people have said and done. The conversation never stops.

At four o'clock Mrs Brown tells Mrs Higgins to bring in the tea. In England making tea is a very serious matter. This is how it is done: fresh water is boiled in a kettle and when the water is hot, a little is put in the tea-pot to warm it. The pot is then dried and the tea put in—one spoonful for each person and 'one for the pot'. When the water is quite boiling it is poured on to the tea and we are told that the tea must be left four or five minutes before it is at its best.

Tea must be poured as carefully as it is made. Some people like to have the milk in the cup first and then the tea, others like to put the tea in first and then add the milk, and others say they cannot tell the difference. Some people do not have milk in their tea at all. When you are pouring tea you should ask each person which he or she prefers. Some people do not like sugar in their tea, others like one, two or three lumps of sugar. Years ago tea used to be served in small china dishes without handles; in those days the word *tea* was pronounced *tay*. Today it is served in thin china cups. Sometimes a silver tea-pot is used, but many people say that tea is best if it is made in a china tea-pot.

Mrs Brown is a good cook—and rather proud of her cooking—so she always serves home-made cakes at her tea-parties. There is also thin bread and butter, and, of course, cigarettes after tea for those who smoke.

When the weather is warm and the sun is shining Mrs Brown serves tea in the garden instead of in the house. The Browns have a big garden round their house, and it is pleasant to sit in the sun or under a tree in the shade. The guests sit on brightly-coloured chairs and the tea is served from little green tables.

About half past four the guests begin to leave. By five o'clock everyone has gone and Mrs Brown can begin to get the evening meal ready for the family. Mrs Brown's Thursday afternoon is rather tiring but she enjoys it all the same.

CONVERSATION

(*It is a quarter to five. All the guests at Mrs Brown's tea-party have left except Mrs Brown's special friend*)

MRS BROWN: Well, that's that for another month. Oh, I am tired.

MRS MORTON: You've been so busy looking after other people you haven't had anything to eat. Pull a chair up to the fire, and I'll pour you another cup of tea. Then I must go.

MRS BROWN: Perhaps I will. You have another cup too. Did you hear Freda Benson ask Betty Richards what they had paid for their house?

MRS MORTON: Yes and Betty told her they had paid six thousand. And I know as a matter of fact they paid only four thousand five hundred.

MRS BROWN: Maud and Pamela seem very friendly now, don't they? A year ago Pamela was going about saying she would never speak to Maud again. She seems to have forgiven her now.

MRS MORTON: Yes. But why did she say that?

MRS BROWN: Because Maud had told someone that Pamela's boy Peter had got his job by saying he had been to a university when he hadn't.

MRS MORTON: Well, did he go to a university?

MRS BROWN: No. But Pamela said he hadn't said he'd been.
But don't let's talk about them any more. I've had
enough for one day. Tell me about your two. Who's
looking after them this afternoon?

MRS MORTON: They're at school until four. Then my mother
said she would come in and get their tea ready. I told
them to be good, and I would be home at five. It's
nearly five now, so I'd better go. They're such a noisy
pair when I'm not there. Thanks for the tea.

MRS BROWN: Thank you for coming. Are you going to
Pamela's on Monday?

MRS MORTON: No. Donald's going to take a day off. He said
he would take me up to London to do some shopping.
We want a new carpet in the sitting-room, so I don't
like to refuse. And I have a birthday next week, so
Donald said I could choose a present.

MRS BROWN: What are you going to have?

MRS MORTON: I don't know. There are such a lot of things I
want. I think I should like a new wrist watch. One of
the children broke mine, and I'm wearing one that
belongs to my mother. Goodness! It's five o'clock. I
really must go. Mother will think I'm never coming.

SENTENCE PATTERNS

25.   *Speak—Talk—Say—Tell*

(a) *Speak*—when words are used by one person.

He spoke for an hour without stopping.
He did not speak a word.
I spoke to him, but he did not answer.
They were all speaking at once, but no one was listening.
He cannot speak English.
I will speak to her about it tomorrow.
He always speaks very quietly.

(b) *Talk*—where two or more people speak and answer each other—a conversation.

He was talking to his friend.
People should not talk in the theatre during the play.
The teacher told the children not to talk in class.
What were they talking about?
They were talking about their holiday.

(c) *Say*—introduces the words spoken.

What did he say?
She said she was going out.
He said "Good morning".
She didn't know what to say.
Don't say anything to him.

(d) *Tell*—to give information.

Tell me what happened.
I told her what I had seen.
We told them about our holiday.
I told the story to the children.
      —to give orders.
Mrs Brown tells her to bring in the tea.
I told him to go away.
Tell him to cut the grass.
We told him not to do it.
She told the taxi-driver to take her home.

26.   Reported Questions and Orders

For Reported Statements and Questions see Sentence Patterns 4 and 5, pages 24–6.

(a) *Reported Questions with* If, Whether

Questions that can have *yes* or *no* for an answer, have *if* or *whether* in the Reported Question form.

"Are you staying in England till Christmas?" he asked.

He asked them if (whether) they were staying in England till
    Christmas.
She asked him if (whether) he would take her home.
He asked me if (whether) I would post the letter.
We asked them if (whether) they would sell their house.
She asked the baker if (whether) he would send the bread.
She asked him if (whether) he would open the door.
He asked her if (whether) she would like to see his new car.
The teacher asked David if (whether) he would play on
    Saturday.

(b) Reported Orders (Imperative)

In Reported Speech the Imperative becomes an infinitive
phrase following a *telling*-verb and a pronoun.

"Go away!" she said.
She told them to go away.

She said "Bring me some tea".
She told him to bring her some tea.

He said to the boy, "Close the door".
He told the boy to close the door.

"Put the car in the garage," she said.
She told him to put the car in the garage.

"Come out of the water," said Mrs Brown.
Mrs Brown told them to come out of the water.

27.   Reported Speech—Summary of Rules

(a) All Reported Speech

Verbs

Where the *saying* verb is Present, Present Perfect or Future
the following verb is unchanged.

Where the *saying* verb is Past, the following verb changes like this:

> Present (Simple or Continuous) becomes
>   Past (Simple or Continuous).
> Present Perfect becomes Past Perfect.
> Past becomes Past Perfect.
> Future becomes Conditional.

Pronouns

First and second person pronouns become third.

Other changes:

this	becomes	that	these	becomes	those
here	„	there	now	„	then
today	„	that day			
yesterday	„	the day before			
tomorrow	„	the next day			
ago	„	before			

(b) *Reported Questions* (Sentence Patterns 5 and 26(*a*), pages 24 and 94).

Where the question begins with a question word (*who, where, how,* etc.) the Reported Question begins with an *asking* verb followed by the question, with the subject before the verb— that is, without inversion.

Where the question does not begin with a question word and could have the answer *yes* or *no*, the Reported Question begins with an *asking* verb followed by *if* or *whether* and the question, with the subject before the verb—that is, without inversion.

(c) *Reported Orders* (*Imperative*) (Sentence Pattern 26(*b*), page 95)

The Reported Imperative begins with a *telling* verb followed by a pronoun and an infinitive phrase.

28. *So—Such a*

We use *So* with adjectives and adverbs, *Such a* with nouns.

(*a*) It is so hot today.
I didn't expect him to be so old.
It is so easy to make a mistake.
It was so kind of you to come.
He always gets so excited.
I'm so sorry I have kept you waiting so long.
Wine is so expensive in England.
I didn't know that he could write so well.
It was so cold that we stayed at home all day.
I was so tired that I went to bed early.

(*b*) It is such a fine day.
We thought he was such a nice man.
It is such a pity it is so cold today.
I have such a lot to do.
It seemed such a long way to the farm.
I didn't know he was such a clever boy.
It's such a long time since we met.
Don't make such a noise.
They have such a nice house in the country.

29. *Used to*

This is used for a customary action in the past.

Used to (ˈjuːstə, ˈjuːstu)
We used to go to London every day.
This is a different verb from *use* (juːz) with its past tense *used* (juːzd).
Mr. Nokes used a quart of green paint.
When we were young, we used to go to the seaside for our holidays.
I used to know him well.

We used to visit her every week.
They used to live next door to us.
You used to be a very nice boy.
She always used to wear smart clothes.
We often used to meet her in town.
I sometimes used to go swimming.
Men used to wear brightly-coloured clothes.
This town used to be quite small.

Negative. Used not, never used to, didn't use to.

Never used to is used with actions that could be repeated:

They used not to come here very often. (They never used to . . .)
They used not to like her.
He used not to do his homework. (He never used to . . .)
We used not to get home till midnight. (We never used to . . .)
He used not to drive a car. (He never used to . . .)
She used not to speak English very well.
He used not to play cricket. (He never used to . . .)
I didn't use to have much money.
There didn't use to be many houses in this road.

Question (Inversions, or with *did*)

Used he to come here every day? (Did he use to . . .?)
Used they to live in Bishopton? (Did they use to . . .?)
Used you to go to the seaside for your holidays? (Did you use to . . .?)
Used people to serve tea in small dishes? (Did people use to . . .?)
Used children in this country to start work at nine years old? (Did children in this country use to . . .?)

Question-tags with *did*

You used to live in London, didn't you?
He used to visit you quite often, didn't he?
They used to go to the seaside each week-end, didn't they?
We used to have an English lesson every morning, didn't we?

NEW WORDS

birthday ('bəɪθdei)
china ('tʃainə)
coal (koul)
fact (fakt)
handle ('handl)
job (dʒob)
lump (lʌmp)
order ('oɪdə)
pair (peə)
pity ('piti)
plan (plan)
shade (ʃeid)
silver ('silvə)
spoonful ('spuɪnful)
tea-pot ('tiɪpot)
wrist (rist)

belong, belonged (bi'loŋ,
  bi'loŋd)

boil, boiled (boil, boild)
forgive, forgave, forgiven
  (fə'giv, fə'geiv, fə'givn)
prefer, preferred (pri'fəɪ,
  pri'fəɪd)
pronounce, pronounced
  (prə'nauns, prə'naunst)
refuse, refused (ri'fjuɪz,
  ri'fjuɪzd)
used (juɪzd)

careless ('keələs)
friendly ('frendli)
home-made ('houm'meid)
own (oun)
proud (praud)
special ('speʃl)
such (sʌtʃ)
tiring ('tairiŋ)

Idioms

to look its best (tə 'luk its 'best)
to leave things about (tə 'liɪv θiŋz ə'baut)
to tell the difference (tə 'tel ðə 'difrəns)
that's that ('ðats 'ðat)
to go about saying . . . (tə 'gou əbaut 'seiiŋ)
to get a job (tə 'get ə 'dʒob)
not to bother about (not tə 'boðər əbaut)
to have enough for one day (tə 'hav inʌf fə 'wʌn 'dei)
as a matter of fact (əz ə 'matər əv 'fakt)
to pull up a chair to the fire (tə 'pul ʌp ə 'tʃeə tə ðə 'faiə)
all the same ('oɪl ðə 'seim)

EXERCISES

A. *Answer these questions in sentences:*

1. On what day does Mrs Brown have her tea-parties?
2. What do people eat at a tea-party?
3. Where does Mrs Brown serve tea in the summer?
4. Why doesn't David like Mrs Brown's tea-parties?
5. How used people to serve tea?
6. Who was looking after Mrs Morton's children?
7. What did Mrs Brown's guests talk about?
8. What did Mrs Morton want for a birthday present?
9. How much did Mrs Richards pay for her house?
10. At what time did the party finish?

B. *Put these sentences into the reported form:*

1. "Who left the door open?" she asked.
2. "Pamela doesn't look very well," Mrs Brown thought.
3. "I should like some new curtains," she said.
4. "Pass me the sugar, please," he said.
5. "Will you take me to town this afternoon?" Susan asked.
6. "How much did the Browns pay for their house?" Mrs Morton asked herself.
7. "Bring me some flowers from the garden, please, Susan," Mrs Brown said.
8. "I think we shall be late," David said.
9. "Don't drive so fast," Mr Brown told David.
10. "Do you think you will like the new carpet?" Mr Brown asked his wife.

C. *Put the verb* talk, speak, say, *or* tell *into these sentences:*

1. No one . . . a word to him.
2. She . . . she did not know what had happened.
3. Mr Brown . . . David to work hard at school.
4. Two or three people were . . . about the party.
5. I can never . . . what he will do next.

6. The child is only five, but he can . . . the time.
7. She was so ill she could not . . .
8. " . . . more loudly. I can't hear what you . . ."
9. Mrs Brown . . . Susan to hurry.
10. He . . . the children a story before they went to sleep.

D. *Write ten sentences about what you did when you were a child. In each sentence use the verb* used to . . .

E. *Add a preposition at the end of these sentences:*
  1. What were you speaking to him . . .?
  2. Which house did she go . . .?
  3. Who was that pen taken . . .?
  4. Which chair was she sitting . . .?
  5. Show me the stairs he fell . . .
  6. Tell me which picture you were looking . . .
  7. What did you do that . . .?
  8. Do you know the woman you were sitting next . . .?
  9. Where did you get that book . . .?
  10. Whose car have they gone to town . . .?

F. *Use these phrases in sentences:*

  make a mistake; many years ago; the same as; three times a day; took great care.

G. *Write five sentences, each using a different adjective with* as . . . as, *and five sentences, each using a different adjective with* than.

  E.g. Bob is as tall as David.
      Birmingham is larger than Cardiff.

H. *Put the word* can, may, *or* should *into these sentences:*
  1. You . . . have those flowers if you want them.
  2. Susan . . . swim very well.
  3. You . . . always look before you cross the road.

4. The child . . . be eleven or twelve, I don't know.
5. Do you know where I . . . find a policeman?
6. Children . . . be seen and not heard.
7. We . . . find mother there when we get home.
8. You . . . pass this examination if you work hard.
9. People . . . think before they speak.
10. You . . . find you have made a mistake.

I. *Change the marked verbs in these sentences into the Past Perfect Tense, and change the other verbs if necessary:*

1. He *finished* his work by six o'clock.
2. We *shall be* in Manchester for a week.
3. He *will do* what they want him to do.
4. It is already Christmas and I *haven't bought* any presents.
5. *Has* he *worked* in this office very long?
6. We *shall not have* any dinner until eight o'clock.
7. I *am meeting* a friend and going shopping with her.
8. It *hasn't been* raining all the morning.
9. I cannot stay in this hotel because I *haven't booked* a room.

J. *Change these reported sentences into the direct form; that is, write the words which were spoken.*

1. She said she had been there for two hours.
2. The manager told Miss Brown to come to work early the next day.
3. The policeman asked him where he was going.
4. David asked Mr Thompson if he was going to London on Thursday.
5. Mrs Brown asked her husband John if he was coming home early.
6. She thought she would buy a new hat.
7. The farmer said he was going to take his pigs to market.
8. The teacher asked the boys where Manchester was.
9. The driver shouted to the boys to be careful.
10. Tom told the Manager that he would like to show his friends round the factory.

K. *Make questions from these sentences:*

   1. She has some apples in her basket.
   2. There was a cow in the field.
   3. He drives a car very well.
   4. He went to Edinburgh last week.
   5. He had finished his work by six o'clock.
   6. They go to the seaside every Sunday.
   7. There are some books on that table.
   8. This house was built a hundred years ago.
   9. The game will be finished before tea-time.
   10. A lot of tea is drunk in this country.

L. *Put the word* much *or* many *into these sentences:*

   1. How . . . boys are there in David's class?
   2. I haven't . . . time for gardening.
   3. You oughtn't to have . . . trouble with a new car.
   4. . . . people go to Switzerland for their holidays.
   5. I don't like . . . sugar or milk in my tea.
   6. I have known him for . . . years.
   7. Is there . . . rain in your country?
   8. He doesn't make . . . mistakes.
   9. Does he know . . . English?
   10. We haven't . . . food in the house.

M. *Put the word* some *or* any *into these sentences:*

   1. Have you . . . money in your pocket?
   2. We met . . . friends at the theatre.
   3. . . . people do not like . . . milk in their tea.
   4. There aren't . . . cakes left.
   5. He threw . . . coal on the fire.
   6. I can't find . . . flowers in the garden.
   7. May I have . . . more bread and butter, please?
   8. Is there . . . bacon in the cupboard?
   9. I have found . . . eggs in the field.
   10. Can you tell me if there are . . . letters for me this morning?

N. *Add an indirect object to these sentences:*

    1. Will you pass . . . that book, please?
    2. David gave . . . a Christmas present.
    3. Did you tell . . . what happened?
    4. We found . . . a new house near London.
    5. Did you send . . . a letter from Edinburgh?
    6. Susan brought . . . some flowers from the garden.
    7. I am going to ask . . . a few questions.
    8. Will you get . . . some shopping from the town?
    9. David would not give . . . any money.
  10. Show . . . what you have in your hand.

O. *Change these sentences into the passive form:*

    1. They have made these bicycles in the factory.
    2. They are building new houses outside the town.
    3. A careless driver was driving that car.
    4. A good teacher will give these lessons.
    5. They make lots of cars in Birmingham.
    6. Someone left a cigarette on the table.
    7. A kind friend gave her that new handbag.
    8. Children think Father Christmas brings their toys.
    9. Mrs Brown invited her to the party.
  10. A friend gave me this gold cigarette-case.

P. *Write five sentences, other than those given in Sentence Pattern*
    18, page 68, *using* Let's.

Q. *Make these sentences negative:*

    1. Tom works on Saturday morning.
    2. Mrs Brown had some friends to tea today.
    3. You must be home by eleven o'clock.
    4. There are some houses for sale in this road.
    5. We shall be in Liverpool next week.
    6. He had some money in his pocket.
    7. I have some sugar in my tea.

8. You ought to go to the theatre every evening.
9. People used to drink tea out of china cups.
10. He knew where he was going.

R. *Describe in your own words how to make a good cup of tea.*

S. *Put the word* when, while, until, after, as soon as, *or* before *into these sentences:*

1. Susan will go straight home . . . she has finished work.
2. Brian wants to be an engineer . . . he grows up.
3. You must stay at home . . . it stops raining.
4. Where did you go . . . you left the theatre?
5. She will go to stay with her sister . . . her husband is abroad.
6. I must finish my work . . . my husband comes home.
7. You should not leave a friend's house . . . a meal is finished.
8. Don't forget to visit Mary . . . you are in London.
9. Children should not speak . . . older people are speaking.
10. He likes to sit in his garden . . . his day's work is done.

A woman was told by her husband to think before she spoke. She answered, "How do I know what I think until I hear what I say?"

LESSON 8

An Evening at the Cinema

DAVID BROWN is a hard worker at school, and his parents hope that he will do well in his examination in the summer, so that he can go up to university next October. He is determined to do his best. But he cannot work all the time, so once or twice a week, when he is tired of work, he goes out with his friend Bob Sandford. They usually go to the theatre or the cinema, but they sometimes go to a dance in Bishopton. They do not often go to a theatre or cinema in London as the cost of the journey and the higher price of seats in London make this too expensive. It is much cheaper in Bishopton.

In England the cinema is usually called 'the pictures'. The American name, 'the movies', is sometimes used. The first performance, or 'showing' as it is called, begins about two o'clock in the afternoon, and the show goes on from then until about half past ten. The cinema is not emptied between the 'showings', so that once you have paid for your seat you can stay in the cinema as long as you like. There are usually one main film, a shorter one, a news film, some advertisements and a 'trailer' telling about the film for the next week. Cinemas used to be more crowded than they are now. Many people used to go to the cinema two or three times a week, but today people like to stay at home to watch television, especially if it is cold and wet outside. The prices of cinema seats outside London are between twenty pence and forty pence. The prices in London are higher.

Cinemas in England are usually larger and more comfortable than the theatres. There is often a restaurant, so that it is possible to spend a pleasant afternoon and evening there. Behind the cinema screen there is a stage, so that the building can be used for concerts and other performances. In some towns in Britain the cinemas are closed on Sundays.

David and Bob enjoy historical films, films about countries very different from their own, crime stories and films that make them laugh. They also like to see foreign films, but it is not often possible to see these in Bishopton. When they were younger they used to enjoy 'cowboy' films, but now they are older they are not so easily satisfied. They do not enjoy these films so much because they find that they are all very much alike. This evening they saw a film of one of Shakespeare's plays. Some famous actors and actresses were in this film. David had seen the play with the same actors and actresses at the Royal Shakespeare Theatre in Stratford-on-Avon the previous summer, so it was interesting to see how the performance in the film was different from the performance on the stage.

The first difference they noticed was that in the film the words of the play became less important and the events became more important. On the stage it did not matter very much where things happened, but in the film places became interesting because they were shown just as they really were. People moved about more in the film: you saw them going from town to town or from country to country. The important people in the film were, of course, the same as in the play, but in the film more was seen of the unimportant people whose names are not known—soldiers, crowds, servants, and so on. The film was very fine and splendid and exciting, but David thought that it had lost something. Much of the poetry of Shakespeare's words had gone, and there were so many people and places and events to watch that you almost forgot the main characters and the really important things that were happening. Telling his father about the film when he got home, David said he thought he would remember the theatre performance he had seen at Stratford long after he had forgotten the film he had seen that evening.

CONVERSATION

(*David has just come home after an evening at the cinema*)

MR BROWN: Hello, David. Have you had a good time?

DAVID: Yes, thanks. Where's Mother?

MR BROWN: She was tired, so she went to bed early. But your supper is laid in the dining-room. We had ours early. What did you think of the film?

DAVID: Very good. I saw the play in Stratford last summer. I was interested to see the difference between the play and the film.

MR BROWN: Which did you like the better?

DAVID: It's hard to say. They'd spent a lot of money on the film and it was very well done. There must have been hundreds of people in it—crowds of people and soldiers and servants. The film moved fast with plenty of things happening all the time. I enjoyed the music and the colour—these were splendid and the photography was very good indeed, but . . .

MR BROWN: But what?

DAVID: Well, something had gone. You didn't notice Shakespeare's words, which are so important in the theatre. And the main characters and what they did and thought didn't seem so clear or stand out as they do in the theatre.

MR BROWN: That's true. I've noticed the same in Shakespeare films that I've seen. After all, the plays were written for the stage—and a very small stage, with nothing on it but the actors, the things they carried in their hands and a few pieces of furniture. So the writer had to put into words all the things that were not there on the stage—what places looked like, the time of day or night, the weather, and so on. The film can show all these things in a way that the stage can never do, even today, so that the words often seem unnecessary. The film speaks to the eye more than to the ear; what we see becomes more important than what we hear.

DAVID: Yes, I think that's it.

MR BROWN: It's easy to find fault, but the film does one good thing: people all over the country can see Shakespeare's plays who wouldn't or couldn't go to see them in the theatre.

DAVID: Yes. I'm glad I saw the film, but I think I shall remember the performance I saw at Stratford long after I have forgotten the film.

SENTENCE PATTERNS

30.   Use of the Articles

(*a*) A noun without an article is used in a general way.
    A noun with the Indefinite Article *a, an* means a single one but not a particular one.
    A noun with the Definite Article *the* refers to some special one or ones.

He likes reading books, but not newspapers.
I want a book from the sitting-room.
Have you seen the book I left on the table?

Do you enjoy wine with your dinner?
We had a good wine with our dinner.
Will you pour the wine, please?

He goes to school every day.
There is a school in most villages in England.
This is the school that my son goes to.

Houses in the middle of towns do not usually have gardens.
They are looking for a new house.
We are looking for the house with the blue door.

She does not smoke cigarettes.
She was smoking a cigarette.
She lit the cigarette he had given her.

Boys are usually taller than girls of the same age.
A boy and a girl were waiting for the bus.
They have two children; the boy is David, the girl is Susan.

Paper is made from wood.
She held a paper in her hand.
The paper in this old book is yellow with age.

Cinemas open at two o'clock in England.
They have built a new cinema in our town.
We went to the cinema in the High Street.

(b) *Countable and Uncountable Nouns* (see Sentence Pattern 7, page 36)

Countable Nouns take an Indefinite Article.
Uncountable nouns do not take an Indefinite Article.

Countable

We saw a dog in the street.
A friend called to see us yesterday.
There was a book on the table.

Uncountable

We all need money.
Corn is made into bread.
A dog eats meat; a horse eats grass.

31.   Participles as Adjectives

He was a worried man.
A burned child is afraid of the fire.
The frightened horse ran away.
The teacher gave them a written exercise.
He left his half-finished meal.
The doctor found the boy had a broken leg.
There was an excited crowd in the street.
At the top of the stairs they found a closed door.
I always enjoy a well-cooked meal.
We met a smartly-dressed woman in town.
There were some uninvited guests at the party.
She has found her long-lost sister.
They came to a half-opened door.
He seemed tired at the end of the day.
She looked worn out by her day's work.
I don't know the way; I think we are lost.

32.   Impersonal Use of *It*

(*a*) *Weather, Temperature, etc.*

It is a fine day today.
It was raining yesterday.
It was cold early this morning.
It is too hot in this room.
It is light earlier in summer than in winter.

(*b*) *Impersonal Subject*

It is easy to find fault.
It is difficult to do this well.
I don't think it is possible to know what people are thinking.
It is impossible to learn English in a few weeks.
It is necessary to think before you speak.
It is dangerous to cross the road without looking.
It is wrong to take what is not yours.
It is right for children to do as they are told.
It is hard to say which I like best.
It seems that I was mistaken.
It is certain that he will be late.
It happened that he had left when I arrived.
It doesn't matter which spoon you use.

33.   *Ago*

Ago means some time in the past, looking back from now. It is used with the past tense.

This happened about a month ago.
The Tower of London was built nearly one thousand years ago.
She called to see me two or three days ago.
He telephoned five minutes ago.
They came to live here more than a year ago.
Two years ago we had a holiday in Wales.
A minute ago you said you were tired.
Not long ago he became manager of the factory.
Many thousands of years ago ice and snow covered the whole of
  Britain.

NEW WORDS

advertisement (əd'vəːtizmənt)
characters ('kariktəz)
cowboy ('kauboi)
crime (kraim)
dance (daːns)
ear (iə)
eye (ai)
fault (fɔːlt)
ice (ais)
parent ('peərənt)
performance (pə'fɔːməns)
photography (fə'tɔgrəfi)
poetry ('pouətri)
screen (skriːn)
servant ('səːvənt)
snow (snou)

determine, determined
  (di'təːmin, di'təːmind)

lay, laid, laid (lei, leid, leid)
satisfy, satisfied ('satisfai,
  'satisfaid)

alike (ə'laik)
clear (kliə)
dangerous ('deindʒərəs)
difficult ('difiklt)
especially (i'speʃli)
famous ('feiməs)
fond (fond)
foreign ('forin)
historical (his'torikəl)
indeed (in'diːd)
impossible (im'posibl)
main (mein)
previous ('priːviəs)
splendid ('splendid)
true (truː)
wet (wet)

Idioms

to do one's best (tə 'duː wʌnz 'best)
as long as you like (əz 'loŋ əz ju 'laik)
to have a good time (tə 'hav ə gud 'taim)
it's hard to say (its 'haːd tə 'sei)
to find fault with (tə 'faind 'fɔːlt wið)

EXERCISES

A. *Answer these questions in sentences:*

  1. How much do the most expensive cinema seats cost
     outside London?
  2. Where is the Royal Shakespeare Theatre?
  3. Give two other names for the cinema.

P.E. II—8

4. What different kinds of films can you see in an English cinema show in one evening?
5. Give the names of two of Shakespeare's plays.
6. Why does David not often go to the cinema in London?
7. What do you think Mr Brown was doing when David got home?
8. Why did Mrs Brown go to bed early?
9. Whom did David go to the pictures with?
10. What else do David and his friend do in the evening?
11. How long ago did Shakespeare live?

B. *Write sentences using the past participles of these verbs as adjectives:*

wave, wear, tear, speak, point, mend, lose, grow, roast, cook.

C. *Write sentences, other than those given in Sentence Pattern 32, using these words with* It:

hot, cold, easy, hard, possible, safe, wrong, early, late, dark, difficult, impossible.

D. *Add a quantity adjective to these sentences:*
1. There are . . . fine shops in London.
2. Is there . . . wine in your glass?
3. How . . . money have you in your pocket?
4. I have had a . . . trouble with this car.
5. This tea is too sweet; you've put too . . . sugar in it.
6. Are there . . . letters for me today?
7. . . . English people like to spend their holidays in Switzerland.
8. There are . . . tigers in England.
9. There were only a . . . people in the restaurant.
10. She asked for . . . more bread and butter.

E. *Use these phrases in sentences:*

in the end; the year before last; just inside the door; how nice; round the corner; a few days ago.

F. *Put the word* should *or* would *into these sentences:*

1. You . . . not come into the house with dirty shoes.
2. I . . . be at work, but I have stayed at home.
3. He said he . . . call to see his friend the next day.
4. Brothers and sisters . . . always help each other.
5. You . . . go to Edinburgh for a holiday.
6. He . . . buy a new car if he had the money.
7. . . . you lend me your pen for a moment, please?
8. You . . . look carefully before you cross the road.
9. . . . you mind if we stayed at home today?
10. He hoped his friend . . . not be late.

G. *Put the word* still *or* yet *into these sentences:*

1. Is it . . . raining?
2. Has the train arrived . . .?
3. Is he . . . working at the same factory?
4. You . . . have a lot of work to do.
5. Have you finished your work . . .?
6. She is . . . trying to learn English.
7. Are they . . . living in the same house?
8. Isn't it dinner time . . .?
9. I think Bob is . . . in London.
10. Has the postman come . . .? No, we are . . . waiting for him.

H. *Add a time preposition to these sentences:*

1. We shan't get to Edinburgh . . . six o'clock.
2. I haven't been in Edinburgh . . . last year.
3. He hasn't been to London . . . six years.
4. Susan doesn't do any work . . . five o'clock.
5. Small children should be in bed . . . eight o'clock.
6. You will be hungry if you go for a walk . . . breakfast.
7. Boys play football . . . winter and cricket . . . summer.
8. I have seen her three or four times . . . the week.
9. The train will arrive . . . five to three.
10. Bus fares will cost more . . . next week.

I. *Put* a *or* the *(if necessary) into these sentences:*

    1. There are a lot of . . . books in this room.
    2. . . . chairs in this room are old.
    3. Many people in England like drinking . . . tea.
    4. Mr Brown bought David . . . bicycle for Christmas.
    5. . . . book I am looking for is a small blue one.
    6. They could not find . . . policeman.
    7. . . . women are usually more interested in clothes than . . . men are.
    8. Susan gets to . . . work at nine each morning.
    9. Tom left . . . factory at six o'clock.
    10. . . . bread is cheap in this country.

J. *Write twelve questions, each beginning with one of these words or phrases:*

    What . . .? When . . .? Why . . .?
    How many . . .?   How old . . .?
    How often . . .?   Who . . .?
    Where . . .?   How much . . .?
    How far . . .?   How long . . .?
              How long ago . . .?

K. *Fill in the spaces in these sentences:*

    1. Mary is not . . . pretty . . . Joan.
    2. David ran . . . fast . . . Bob.
    3. Edinburgh is one of the . . . beautiful cities in Britain.
    4. This exercise is easier . . . the last one.
    5. Some books are . . . interesting . . . others.
    6. This was . . . cheapest hat in the shop.
    7. Is Edinburgh . . . large . . . London?
    8. She bought the . . . expensive car she could find.
    9. I don't think Bob is . . . clever . . . David.
    10. Trains usually go . . . quickly . . . buses.

L. *Give the opposites to these adjectives:*

easy; white; open; good; polite; happy; clean; large; big; many.

Now use each of your words in a separate sentence.

M. *Rewrite these sentences in the passive:*

1. Someone has cut the grass in the garden.
2. The car took them to the theatre.
3. Mr Jones has given a present to the children.
4. Someone will take the children home by car.
5. People will remember this play for a long time.
6. Did David break this window?
7. Is Mr Nokes doing this work?
8. Has anyone found my pen yet?
9. Has anyone eaten those chocolates?
10. A friend of mine wrote this letter to me.

N. *Put one of these adverbs into the right place in each of these sentences:*

always; never; sometimes; often; usually; almost.

1. I have sugar in my tea.
2. It is warm in summer.
3. Mrs Brown goes to tea with her friends.
4. I have finished my work.
5. David is not ill.
6. Tom works on Saturday afternoon.
7. Some people say that in England it rains.
8. In England we have snow in July.
9. It is warm in July in England.
10. Children should cross the road without looking.

O. *Write* in your own words *a paragraph about the difference between a play in the theatre and a film of it at the cinema.*

P. *Write a letter to a friend telling about a film you have seen lately.*

Q. *Use* little, less *or* few *in these sentences:*

1. They are very fond of their nice . . . house.
2. I think there are a . . . cakes in that box.
3. You will have . . . trouble with a new car than with an old one.
4. There is very . . . bread in the house.
5. We have . . . garden than the Browns.
6. Mr Brown stayed a . . . days with his friend.
7. We drink . . . wine than some of our friends do.
8. We have . . . time left before the end of the holiday.
9. There are still a . . . flowers in the garden.
10. He earns . . . money than his brother does.

R. *Put the right prepositions into these sentences:*

1. Cricket is a very different game . . . football.
2. If you are not careful you will fall . . . the water.
3. The child fell . . . the stairs and broke his arm.
4. He threw the cigarette . . . the window.
5. This train arrives . . . Liverpool . . . six o'clock.
6. Do you know which platform the train starts . . .?
7. Sunday is the day that comes . . . Saturday and Monday.
8. It is harder going . . . the mountain than coming . . .
9. You should not go out on a cold morning . . . a coat.

S. *Put the word* before, since, *or* ago *into these sentences:*

1. Have you been to England . . .?
2. He has lived here . . . last October.
3. I have never seen him . . .
4. This all happened a long time . . .
5. Six years . . . I bought this house, and we've lived here ever . . .
6. He lived in London . . . he came here.
7. How long . . . did you buy that car?
8. I have had this car . . . last summer.
9. Mr Brown visited Edinburgh many years . . .
10. David had visited Oxford three weeks . . .

LESSON 9

The Big Stores

SUSAN has done a lot of extra work in her office lately, and Mr Robinson, the Manager, has given her two days' holiday, so she and her mother have come up to London for a day's shopping. Spring has come at last, and Susan wants some new clothes. Mrs Brown would be sorry if she hadn't a daughter because she likes to have someone to go shopping with. Today they are enjoying themselves very much.

After Mr Brown had gone to work and David had gone to school, they tidied the house and then caught an early train to London. They were in Oxford Street just after ten, with all the day in front of them. They did the important shopping first: Susan bought a light spring coat and two pairs of shoes, and Mrs Brown bought some shirts and underclothes for David. Now they are having lunch in the restaurant of one of the big stores.

These stores are wonderful places. It is easy to understand why people enjoy shopping here. They sell everything, so that you could stay here all day if you wanted to. Some women do nothing but walk round all day, doing their shopping under one roof. These big stores started in America, and the idea was brought to this country by Gordon Selfridge about fifty years ago. Selfridge's is still one of the biggest stores in London; other big stores are Harrods and Gamages. All the things for sale are on the counters so that they can be easily seen, and the customers walk round and choose what they want. Indeed, if you like you can walk round the store without buying anything at all.

The store is divided into departments: women's clothes, men's clothes, shoes, toys, sports goods, umbrellas, leather goods, china and glass, food and so on. There are lifts to take people to the different floors. There is a big restaurant with an orchestra and sometimes a tea-room as well. There is a room where you can write letters and a post office to post them. You will also find a room where you can rest if you are tired. There are men's and women's hairdressers and an office where you book seats for the theatre or arrange to travel anywhere in the world.

Now Mrs Brown and her daughter have finished their lunch and are ready to start shopping again. There are lots of little things that Mrs Brown wants for the house, and Susan is going to buy a birthday present for a girl in her office. They may see one or two suitable things as they walk round and, unless these are too expensive, they will buy them. Last of all Mrs Brown will buy something ready-cooked from the food department to make a quick meal for the family when she gets home.

After a hurried cup of tea they will take a taxi to Victoria Station and, if they are lucky, they will be home before Mr Brown gets back from the office. A tiring day, but enjoyable —if you like shopping!

CONVERSATION

(In the restaurant at the big store)

MRS BROWN: Oh dear, I'm glad to sit down. We must have walked miles.

SUSAN: Yes, I'm ready to sit down, too. But it would be worse if the weather were hot. And we've almost finished now. What are you going to have for lunch?

MRS BROWN: What is there? Let me see.

SUSAN: I think I shall have soup, and roast beef. I'm hungry.

MRS BROWN: I don't want soup. I shall have fruit juice and chicken.

(They give their order to the waitress)

MRS BROWN: Well, are you pleased with your morning's shopping?

SUSAN: Yes, I think so. I've spent more money than I wanted to, but that can't be helped. The coat was very expensive.

MRS BROWN: I think you did well to get that one. The colour's right for this time of year and it fits you beautifully. I don't think they charged you too much.

SUSAN: I hope those brown shoes will fit me. They seemed a little small when I tried them on, but they were a good bargain, and fashionable, too.

MRS BROWN: I daresay they'll fit better when you've worn them. Now, let me see: what must I buy this afternoon? I've got David's shirts and some underclothes. Then your father wants some socks and some handkerchiefs

—he does nothing but grumble if there aren't enough clean handkerchiefs.

SUSAN: And I want a present. It's Anne Miller's birthday on Friday.

MRS BROWN: How much are you going to pay?

SUSAN: I think I can afford about fifty pence, but I must buy something nice.

MRS BROWN: Well, we can get all these in the store here.

SUSAN: Oh, and Tom asked me to book seats for the play at the Haymarket. He's taking me to see it on Saturday week.

· · · ·

(*At the Browns' home that evening*)

MR BROWN (*who has just come in*): Well, did you finish your shopping? Has anyone any money left?

SUSAN: Not a penny. You'll have to lend me some till Friday. But we got what we wanted.

MRS BROWN: And we were home in time to get dinner ready for you. But after dinner I'm going to sit by the fire and don't dare ask me to move till bed-time. We've done nothing but walk all day long. I believe we've walked miles! And what crowds of people! I'm tired out.

SENTENCE PATTERNS

34.   Conditional Sentences

Conditional clauses usually begin with *if*. In the negative, *if not* is usually expressed by *unless*.

(*a*) In this kind of sentence, the speaker is saying what will follow if a stated event happens, but he does not know whether it will happen or not.

Notice that the *if* clause has the verb in the Present Tense.

If Susan meets Tom in town he will take her for tea.
If it doesn't rain, I shall go to the seaside tomorrow.
If he comes in time we shall catch the train.
If you have finished your work you may go home.
If he has time he will call to see his friend.
Mrs Brown will be angry if her husband is late for dinner.
David will be pleased if he passes his examination.
I shall buy a new coat if I can afford it.
You'll fall out of the window if you're not careful.
He can come in our car if there is room.

He can't go unless his mother says he may.
You can't drive a car alone in England unless you have passed
   a test.
I shan't go to the party unless I am invited.
David won't pass his examination unless he works hard.
He won't eat his dinner unless it is well cooked.
I shall be in London by six o'clock unless I miss the train.

(b) In this kind of sentence the speaker is stating what would
   probably follow if an imagined event should happen. The
   imagined event may be possible or impossible.
   Notice the use of the Past Tense in the conditional part of
   the sentence, and the use of *were* for *was* (*if I were you*).

I should go if I were you. (But I'm not)
He would buy these if he had enough money. (But I don't
   know whether he has or not)
I should stay in England another year if I could. (But I can't)
He would learn more quickly if he worked harder. (But he
   won't)
I shouldn't give him so much money if he were my son. (But
   he isn't)
If they lived in London they would earn more money. (But
   they don't)
If the sun were shining we should go for a picnic. (But it
   isn't)

If he spoke to me like that I should be angry. (But he doesn't)
If I had a car I would take you to the station. (But I haven't)
If she bought fewer clothes she would have more money.
(But she won't)

(c) In this kind of sentence the speaker makes a general statement
which is true at all times:
In these sentences *when* can usually be used for *if*.

If it is fine we go out in the car.
If boys work hard their parents are pleased.
If you drop china on the floor it breaks.
If people eat too much they get fat.
Susan enjoys swimming if the weather is warm.
Mrs Brown goes to bed early if she is tired.
People go to the doctor if they are ill.
Mr Brown does not like tea if there is too much sugar in it.

35.   Possessive of Nouns

To show possession in nouns we add *'s*. If the noun already ends
in *s*, we add ' only.

The boy's book (boy + 's)
The boys' books (boys + ')
The child's toy (child + 's)
The children's toys (children + 's)
The lady's coat (lady + 's)
The ladies' coats (ladies + ')
The man's shoes (man + 's)
The men's shoes (men + 's)
St. Anne's Church (St. Anne + 's)

She goes to a girls' school (girls + ')
This factory makes men's and women's clothes (men + 's,
women + 's)
They went to Mrs Brown's tea-party (Mrs Brown + 's)
We visited the Browns' house in Bishopton (Browns + ')

The manager's desk was a large one (manager + 's)
We met the policemen's wives (policemen + 's)
They had three weeks' holiday (weeks + ')

Because most plural nouns end in *s*, most possessive plurals add
' only.

A few well-known names ending in *s* sometimes add *'s* in the
possessive.

E.g. Charles's book. St James's Church.

Of should generally be used instead of *'s* for possession, when
speaking of things which are not alive:

E.g. The dog's back.   The back of the book.
     The boy's foot.   The foot of the page.

Where there are two or more nouns together, which are names for
the same person or thing, the last one takes the *'s.*

My son John's bicycle.

Jones the baker's van.

(But in "Tom, the piper's son," *Tom* and *the piper* are two
different people, so there is a comma after *Tom.*)

36.   *Dare*

Dare has three meanings:

(*a*) To be brave enough to do something.

In the Present Tense, the negative and interrogative are
formed without *do* and are followed by an infinitive without
to and the third person singular has *dare* without *s*.

They dare to say I did it!
He dares to say he doesn't know me!
She dares to speak to me after what happened last week!
You dare to tell me you have spent all my money!

I daren't drive as fast as he does.
We daren't tell you what happened.
He daren't ask his father for more money.
They daren't let their dog out of the garden.

Dare he jump from that wall?
Dare you tell him he's wrong?
Dare she travel so far by herself?
How dare you speak to me so rudely!
How dare he say such things about us!

In the Past Tense, the interrogative is formed with *do*, the negative either with or without *do*. The infinitive may be with or without *to*.

They dared (to) ask me how much money I had.
He dared (to) jump into the sea to help his friend.
No one dared (to) say a word.

Did you dare go into the dark house alone?
Did he dare ask you for money?
Did she dare live in the house alone?
We daren't tell him what happened.
She daren't go out in the cold all last winter.
He didn't dare ask her for her telephone number.

(*b*) To challenge someone to do something. Here the negative and interrogative are formed with *do*, and *dare* is followed by a direct object and an infinitive with *to*.

I dare you to say that again.
She dared him to drive at eighty miles an hour.
We dared him to do his worst.

Did he dare you to jump off the bridge?
Do you dare me to hit that policeman?
I didn't dare him to do such a silly thing.

(*c*) *Daresay*. This is written as one word and means *I think, I expect, very likely*. It is used in the first person singular only.

I daresay you're right.
I daresay she'll write to you next week.

Will he be home in time for Christmas? I daresay (he will).
I daresay you know what you're doing, but be careful.

37·   *Nothing but*

He is learning nothing but English.
The child does nothing but play all day.
I am telling you nothing but the truth.
They buy nothing but the best butter.
We have had nothing but trouble since he arrived.
I can give you nothing but bread and cheese.
We have had nothing to eat all day but a piece of bread.

NEW WORDS

bargain ('baɪgin)
department (di'paɪtmənt)
goods (gudz)
hairdresser ('heədresə)
juice (dʒuɪs)
leather ('leðə)
magazine (magə'ziɪn)
sock (sok)
sport (spoɪt)
test (test)
underclothes ('ʌndəklouðz)

afford, afforded (ə'foɪd,
    ə'foɪdid)
arrange, arranged (ə'reindʒ,
    ə'reindʒd)
bark, barked (baɪk, baɪkt)
believe, believed (bi'liɪv,
    bi'liɪvd)
charge, charged (tʃaɪdʒ,
    tʃaɪdʒd)

dance, danced (daɪns, daɪnst)
dare, dared (deə, deəd)
daresay (deə'sei)
divide, divided (di'vaid,
    di'vaidid)
grumble, grumbled ('grʌmbl,
    'grʌmbld)
lend, lent (lend, lent)

beautifully ('bjuɪtifli)
easily ('iɪzili)
enjoyable (ən'dʒoiəbl)
extra ('ekstrə)
fashionable ('faʃnəbl)
lately ('leitli)
lucky ('lʌki)
quick (kwik)
suitable ('sjuɪtəbl)
unless (ən'les)

Idioms

to enjoy oneself (tu inˈdʒoi wʌnˈself)
with all the day in front of them (wið ˈɔːl ðə ˈdei in ˈfrʌnt əv
    ðəm)
it can't be helped (it ˈkɑːnt bi ˈhelpt)
to try something on (tə ˈtrai ˈsʌmθiŋ ˈon)
let me see (ˈlet mi ˈsiː)
he does nothing but grumble (hi dʌz ˈnʌθiŋ bət ˈgrʌmbl)
to be tired out (tə bi ˈtaiəd ˈaut)

EXERCISES

A. *Dictation*

    People enjoy shopping at the big stores because they can
get everything they want under one roof. If you want
to buy children's shoes, a man's overcoat, a lady's umbrella,
some new furniture, a boy's football, a saucepan for the
kitchen, and a baby's toy, you do not have to go to seven
different shops. In most of these stores you can also have a
meal in the restaurant, write letters and post them, book
seats for the theatre, have your hair cut, or rest in an arm-
chair if you are tired. I daresay you have shops like this in
your own country; perhaps in your country they are even
bigger. But in each country, things are different, so next
time you are in London, I should visit one of the big stores
there, if I were you.

B. *Answer these questions in sentences:*

  1. Why did Susan have two days' holiday from work?
  2. Why was Mrs Brown enjoying her day in London?
  3. What did Mrs Brown buy for her husband?
  4. Who first started the big stores in England?
  5. What can you do in a big store as well as shopping?
  6. Why did Mrs Brown buy some food in the store to take
     home with her?
  7. What did Susan have for lunch?

8. What had Tom asked Susan to do?

9. What was the name of the girl in her office for whom Susan was buying a present?

10. About what time did Susan and Mrs Brown get home?

C. *Put a form of the verb* talk, speak, say, *or* tell *into these sentences:*

1. She smiled at him but she didn't . . . anything.

2. Please can you . . . me the time?

3. At a party some people like to stand and . . .

4. He can only . . . a few words of English.

5. We will wait and hear what they . . .

6. I could not . . . for laughing.

7. They would not . . . us what had happened.

8. "What a lovely day!" she . . .

9. I . . . to the driver, but he took no notice.

10. I don't know what you are . . . about.

11. You can never . . . what will happen next.

12. The three men . . . together for more than an hour.

D. *Write a composition on* A Day's Shopping. *The Conversation passage will help you.*

E. *Write down, in three lists, the subjects, verbs and objects in these sentences:*

1. Three men were eating their lunch in the hotel.

2. Where have you put my coat?

3. Most people like sugar in their tea.

4. Susan hasn't visited London for six months.

5. Mary bought some ties and handkerchiefs in the store.

6. Have you seen my brother this week?

7. Mr and Mrs Brown have bought a new house in Bishopton.

8. Schoolboys do not play football in summer.

9. Tom slept all through the church service.

10. You can't leave your car here.

P.E. II—9

F. *State whether the verb* have *in each of the following sentences means possession, obligation, or a customary habit:*

1. I have an egg for breakfast every morning.
2. We have to go home now.
3. She has a new hat every fortnight.
4. He has a new car.
5. You have to drive carefully in a crowded street.
6. I have ten pence in my pocket.
7. David will have to buy a lot of books at his university.
8. We have a dance here once a week.
9. You will have to learn to dance better than that.
10. We have a lot of rain in this country.

G. *Rewrite the sentences in Exercise F in the negative.*

H. *Give short answers to the following questions, first in the affirmative and then in the negative:*

1. Has Tom Smith bought a new car?
2. Do you like gardening?
3. Can you come to London tomorrow ?
4. Does she like shopping?
5. Is she staying in England long?
6. Has this play been acted before?
7. Have you a watch?
8. Ought I to finish my homework?
9. May I close the window, please?
10. Have the letters arrived yet?

I. *Put these sentences into the singular:*

1. They do their work well.
2. The men will finish their work soon.
3. They know what will happen if they make a mistake.
4. Your friends can't stay here.
5. These knives don't cut very well.
6. Every time children cross the road they should look both ways.

7. Have they finished their breakfast yet?
8. The boys play cricket in summer, but in the winter they play football.
9. Are your friends going to Greece next week, or haven't they made up their minds yet?
10. Their friends have given them some books and magazines to read in the train.

J. *Put the verbs in brackets into the correct Present Tense:*

1. He (*travel*) to London by train every day.
2. He usually (*go*) by bus, but today he (*go*) by train.
3. People who (*live*) in glass houses should not throw stones.
4. They (*buy*) a new house next month.
5. David (*sit*) at the table but I don't know if he (*do*) his homework.
6. In the winter I (*wear*) a heavy coat, but today I (*wear*) a light suit.
7. Every morning he (*wake*) at seven o'clock.
8. Their dog (*bark*) every night and it (*bark*) now.
9. She (*stay*) with her friends in Edinburgh for a few days.
10. Children (*run*) to their mothers when they (*hurt*) themselves.

K. *Put the verb into the correct tense:*

1. If you hurry you (*catch*) the train.
2. You will be too warm if you (*wear*) a coat.
3. If you (*keep*) your money you would have more in the bank.
4. We (*invite*) you to stay if we had a larger house.
5. Mrs Brown (*go*) to see her sister if she (*need*) a rest.
6. Susan (*like*) to swim in the sea if the sun (*shine*).
7. You would learn English more quickly if you (*listen*) to English people.
8. You can't buy these books unless you (*have*) enough money.

    9. David will not be satisfied unless he (*pass*) his examination.

  10. You shouldn't go out unless you (*finish*) your work.

L. *Put these phrases into the possessive form without* of *or* for:

    1. The friends of our wives.
    2. The palace of King Charles.
    3. The poems of Keats.
    4. The house of the Browns.
    5. A school for boys.
    6. A hairdresser for ladies.
    7. The shoes of the men.
    8. The books of the children.
    9. The Palace of St James.
  10. The sword of the King.

M. *Answer these questions in complete sentences:*

    1. Where did you buy that book?
    2. How many times have you been to England?
    3. When did you start learning English?
    4. Why have you come to this class?
    5. How much did that book cost?
    6. How much money have you spent this week?
    7. How much money did you spend last week?
    8. What did you do last Sunday?
    9. How old were you on your last birthday?
  10. What did Susan buy at the big store?

N. *Write ten sentences, each using a word for a part of the body.*

O. *Add to each of the following sentences a statement beginning with* so *or* neither:

    1. Tom likes to go to the theatre.
    2. My friend has been in England for six months.
    3. Mr Brown doesn't like much sugar in his tea.
    4. You must go home now.

5. They haven't had their lunch yet.
6. Schoolboys have holidays in the summer.
7. My son was here last night.
8. Susan finishes work at five o'clock.
9. Tom can swim very well.
10. We needn't go home yet.

P. *Write a composition on* My Mother.

Q. *Put these sentences into reported speech following a verb in the Past Tense:*

1. I found the book on the table.
2. We are living in London.
3. I can swim but I can't drive a car.
4. I don't go to London very often.
5. We have lived in England all our lives.
6. I've had my lunch.
7. I'm not a very good footballer.
8. Tom has finished his work.
9. There are several books on the table.
10. We stayed in Manchester for a week.

How was He?

Moses was the son of Pharaoh's daughter and the daughter of Pharaoh's son.

Can you explain this?

explain (ik'splein)   Moses ('mouzəz)   Pharaoh ('feərou)

LESSON 10

A Family Birthday

AT the end of March it will be David's eighteenth birthday. When the children were younger Mrs Brown used to arrange a birthday party for them, to which their friends were invited. The parties were noisy and Mrs Brown found them very tiring. She was glad when the children grew up and something else could be arranged instead. Now Mr and Mrs Brown take the children to the theatre or out to dinner when a birthday comes round.

Susan wants to buy David a birthday present. She knows he likes to go camping in the summer with his friends and he wants a new tent. She tried to get one in Bishopton, but she could not find the one she wanted. Then one morning a firm in the North of England advertised tents for sale and Susan saw the advertisement in a newspaper. She decided to order one by post. This is the letter she wrote:

Oak Tree House,
Felton Road,
Bishopton,
Surrey.
10th March, 1970

Messrs Harris & Co., Ltd,
Market Street,
Leeds, 1.

Dear Sirs,

   I wish to order a small tent, size 6ft. × 3ft., No. X 152 as advertised in the "Daily Post" of 10th March.

  I enclose a Money Order for £5 to cover cost and carriage.

Yours faithfully,
Susan Brown

Two days later Susan received a letter from the firm in Leeds. The address on the envelope was set out like this:

Miss S. Brown,
  Oak Tree House,
    Felton Road,
      BISHOPTON, Surrey

and this is the letter:

JOHN HARRIS & CO. LTD,

Market Street,

Leeds, 1.

DB/JS   11th March 1970

Miss S. Brown,
Oak Tree House,
Felton Road,
BISHOPTON, Surrey.

Dear Madam,

Thank you for your letter of 10th March, ordering a tent No. X 152, and for the enclosed Money Order.

We have today sent the tent to you by parcel post, and hope that you will find it satisfactory.

Yours faithfully,

Douglas Barton

Sales Manager

The tent came by parcel post the same day, and Susan hid it in a cupboard so that David would not see it.

When David's birthday arrived, the post brought him many presents from his friends and relations. Most of the presents from his family were beside his plate at the breakfast-table and the family all wished him a happy birthday. It was a week-day, so everyone went off to school or work after breakfast, but it was arranged that Mrs Brown, Susan and David would meet Mr Brown for dinner at a London restaurant and go on to a theatre afterwards. They had an excellent dinner, during which they drank David's health and again wished him a happy birthday. The play was clever and amusing and when they returned home on a late train they all agreed that it had been a most enjoyable evening.

CONVERSATION

*(David, who has woken up late this morning, comes downstairs
and finds the rest of the family at breakfast)*

SUSAN: Hello, David. Many happy returns of the day.

MRS BROWN: Happy birthday, dear. It seemed a pity to wake
you.

MR BROWN: I suppose we mustn't blame you for coming
down late on your birthday. Many happy returns.

DAVID: Thank you, all of you. Has the post come?

MRS BROWN: Yes. The letters and parcels are on the table
by the front door.

DAVID: Are there many?

MRS BROWN: Quite a lot. Now, have your breakfast, and
open your letters and parcels after.

SUSAN: What are we going to do this evening? I suppose
David's going to take us out with all the money he's got
for his birthday.

DAVID: I'm saving up for the summer holidays. I haven't a
boy-friend to pay for me, like some people I know.

MRS BROWN: Now, you two, don't quarrel!

MR BROWN: I've booked seats for the theatre. I thought we
could all meet and have dinner first. Is that all right,
David?

DAVID: Very good indeed. What are we going to see?

MR BROWN: I thought you would enjoy the new play
Information Received. My newspaper said it was funny
as well as exciting.

MRS BROWN: I think we shall all like that. What do you say,
David? It's your birthday.

DAVID: Thank you. That's fine. Now, I think I'll open my
presents.

•   •   •   •

(*Later at a restaurant in London, the Browns are enjoying a good meal. There is a bottle of wine in ice on the table and everyone is all smiles*)

MRS BROWN: Well, I am enjoying my dinner, John. And I like this place. Why haven't we been here before?

MR BROWN: I'm glad you like it. I wanted to find somewhere we hadn't been to so I asked Norman Bentley. He and his wife dine out a lot. And he recommended this place. He's seldom wrong about food and drink.

SUSAN: Is he the man you sometimes go fishing with?

MR BROWN: Yes. And a very good fisherman he is, too.

DAVID: What you can see in fishing . . .

MRS BROWN: Now, David, it may be your birthday, but it doesn't mean you can start making fun of your father.

MR BROWN: Let me tell you, if someone hadn't caught it, you wouldn't have had that excellent fish you've just eaten with so much enjoyment.

MRS BROWN: John, isn't it time we drank David's health?

MR BROWN: You're right as usual, my dear. Waiter!

(*The waiter uncorks the bottle and pours the wine*)

MR BROWN: Well, boy, here's to your very good health!

MRS BROWN: Happy birthday, dear!

SUSAN: Cheers! Do you want to make a speech?

DAVID: No, I don't. But thank you all the same. I can hardly drink to my own health, but I'm not going to miss my share of the wine. Cheers!

MR BROWN: I suppose the next time your birthday comes round, David, you'll be at Oxford.

MRS BROWN: That reminds me. There are lots of things you'll want for your rooms, David. I'm going to have a busy time getting everything ready.

SUSAN: Poor father. These expensive sons.

DAVID: Well, it won't cost as much as a daughter's wedding.

SUSAN: Who said anything about a wedding?

DAVID: All right! All right! Don't get excited. These things do happen.

MRS BROWN: Now you two. This is David's birthday and not the time to argue.

WAITER: Would you like coffee, sir?

MR BROWN: Please.

WAITER (*to Mrs Brown, pouring the coffee*): Black or white, madam?

MRS BROWN: Black, please.

• • • •

MR BROWN: And now I think we must go. We don't want to be late for the theatre.

MRS BROWN: No. I don't like rushing in at the last minute; I like to be in my seat well before the curtain goes up.

MR BROWN: The theatre is only just round the corner, so we shan't want a taxi.

SENTENCE PATTERNS

38.   Special Verbs

There are twelve verbs in English which are different from all other verbs. (They are sometimes called *anomalous finites*.) These verbs are:

Be (am, is, are, was, were)
Have (has, have, had)
Do (do, does, did)
Shall (shall, should)
Will (will, would)
Can (can, could)
May (may, might)
Ought
Must
Need
Dare
Used

(a) Difference of Special Verbs

They are different from other verbs because:

(i) they form the negative by adding *not* (or the shortened form *n't*) instead of using *do not*.

He isn't a very good driver.
They haven't a house of their own.
I shan't be long.
He won't work hard at school.
The small child cannot tell the time.
He may not arrive till tomorrow.
You oughtn't to do that.
He needn't come if he is tired.
I daren't speak to him after what has happened.

(ii) they form the interrogative by inversion (putting the verb before the subject) instead of by using *do*.

Is he a clever boy?
Have you a match, please?
Shall I open the window?
Will you pass me the sugar?
Can they speak English?
May I come in?
Ought he to stay up so late?
Must you go home now?
Need I answer his letter?
Dare you swim in that cold water?
Used they to come here often?

(b) Uses of special verbs

These special verbs have many uses. Among these are:

(i) as auxiliaries to form compound tenses.

She is living in Bishopton.
He was working in London.
They have gone to London.
He had finished his work.

I shall stay here till next Monday.
It will be fine tomorrow.

(ii) to save repetition by forming short answers to questions.

Is she a good swimmer? Yes, she is.
Have they finished their dinner? Yes, they have.
Shall we be late? Yes, we shall.
Will they meet you at the station? Yes, they will.
Can she swim? No, she can't.
May we go home now? Yes, you may.
Oughtn't he to be more careful? Yes, he ought.
Must I do my homework? Yes, you must.
Need I finish this tonight? No, you needn't.
Dare you drive at that high speed? No, I daren't.

All other verbs form short answers with *do*.

Do you work in Birmingham? Yes, I do.
Do you often come to London? No, I don't.

(iii) to form question-tags.

He isn't ready yet, is he?
They haven't arrived yet, have they?
You don't live in Leeds, do you?
We shall be home before morning, shan't we?
Tom can stay to tea, can't he?
She may pick some flowers, mayn't she?
He ought to speak more politely, oughtn't he?
He must wash his hands before tea, mustn't he?
He needn't go to bed yet, need he?

All other verbs form question-phrases with *do*. (See Sentence Pattern 39 on page 143.)

(iv) after *so* and *neither* (*nor*) in additions to statements.

He's a good swimmer. So am I.
I've finished my work. So has he.
She doesn't work on Saturday. Neither do I.
He won't go there for a holiday again. Nor shall I.
I can't come tomorrow, nor can Tom.
They must work hard this term. So must we.

(v) The special verb *do* is used to form the negative and interrogative of other verbs.

He doesn't like living in the country.
I didn't go to London yesterday.
They don't come to see us often.
Did you enjoy your holiday in Ireland?
Does she work in your office?
Do they live near you?

(vi) To express the following ideas:

Ability (can)

Tom can drive a car well.
Susan can type letters quickly.

Permission (may, can)

May I go home now?
May I stay to lunch?
Can I come in?
Can I sit here, please?

Possibility (may)

It may rain tomorrow.
He may be a great man some day.

Obligation (must, ought, need, should, have to)

You must go home now.
You ought to be more careful.
Need I go to bed yet?
People should think before they speak.
We have to go now.

Possession (have)

I have a book in my hand.

(c) *Verbs which are both special and ordinary verbs*

Some of these special verbs are sometimes used as ordinary verbs, and then they form their negative and interrogative with *do* as other ordinary verbs.

(i) *Have* (customary)

We don't have much snow in this country.
I don't have sugar in my tea.
Do you have a bath every day?

(ii) *Do* (perform)

We don't do very much on Sundays.
He didn't do his homework last night.
Did you do that exercise yourself?
What does he do for a living?

(iii) *Need* (require)

You don't need a new book yet.
I don't need your help, thank you.
Do you need a new book?
Do we need a fire in this warm weather?

(iv) *Dare* (challenge)

He didn't dare anyone to do it.
Did she dare you to do it?

39.   Question-Tags

An affirmative statement is followed by a negative question-tag,
and expects the answer *Yes*.
He's going to London tomorrow, isn't he?

A negative statement is followed by an affirmative question-tag,
and expects the answer *No*.
He isn't going to London tomorrow, is he?

The 'special' verbs are repeated in the question-tag, whether
they are used alone or as auxiliaries.
He can swim well, can't he?
He is tall, isn't he?

Other verbs have *do* in the question-tag.
He works hard, doesn't he?

(a) *Affirmative Statement, expecting answer* Yes.

(i) *Special Verbs*

David is too old for a children's party, isn't he?
Tom can swim well, can't he?
People must drive carefully in towns, mustn't they?
David ought to go to bed before midnight, oughtn't he?
We may leave our car here without lights, mayn't we?
We shall meet again next week, shan't we?
You've lost your way, haven't you?
He'll finish his work before lunch, won't he?

(ii) *Other Verbs*

The Browns spent a very pleasant evening, didn't they?
David enjoyed his dinner, didn't he?
Susan likes a day in London, doesn't she?
David plays football on Saturdays doesn't he?

(b) *Negative Statements, expecting answer* No.

(i) *Special Verbs*

You daren't jump off that high wall, dare you?
We needn't go home yet, need we?
You won't be home too late, will you?
Tom hasn't been to Switzerland before, has he?
They aren't living in Bishopton now, are they?

(ii) *Other Verbs*

Susan didn't write to Tom yesterday, did she?
You didn't take my book from the table, did you?
They don't live in Paris now, do they?
Mrs Brown doesn't drive the car, does she?

40.   Two forms of the Shortened Negative

The shortened negative has two forms:

He isn't very clever.
or He's not very clever.
It isn't Wednesday today.
or It's not Wednesday today.
We aren't going to the theatre this evening.

or We're not going to the theatre this evening.
  They aren't living here now.
or They're not living here now.
  Mr Brown hasn't finished his work yet.
or Mr Brown's not finished his work yet.
  I haven't seen him since last Tuesday.
or I've not seen him since last Tuesday.
  Susan hasn't eaten her breakfast.
or Susan's not eaten her breakfast.
  It hasn't rained at all this week.
or It's not rained at all this week.
  You haven't brushed your hair.
or You've not brushed your hair.
  They haven't sold their house.
or They've not sold their house.
  I hadn't seen him before.
or I'd not seen him before.
  He hadn't been to London.
or He'd not been to London.
  They hadn't had any breakfast.
or They'd not had any breakfast.
  I shan't answer his letter.
or I'll not answer his letter.
  David won't catch that train.
or David'll not catch that train.
  It won't rain tomorrow.
or It'll not rain tomorrow.
  We won't listen to her.
or We'll not listen to her.
  They won't be here till this evening.
or They'll not be here till this evening.

41.   *Like—Want—Wish*

(*a*) *Like* means to take pleasure in, to be pleased with.

  I like a lot of sugar in my tea.
  Do you like my new hat?

She likes an egg for breakfast every morning.
We like to spend our holidays in Switzerland.
He likes to go to bed early.
They don't like living in the country.
Do you like swimming?
Mr Brown doesn't like walking to the station.

(b) *Want* means to desire.

Does he want any more wine?
He wants a new bicycle.
I want a box of matches, please.
Do you want to go to the theatre this evening?
I want to see you as soon as possible.
Susan wants to buy a present for her friend.

Should like or *would like* is sometimes used as a polite form of *want:*

I should like another cup of tea, please.
Would you like a cigarette?
We should very much like to meet your friend.
Would you like to read this letter?
They would like to stay to tea.
Where would you like to go for your holidays?
Would you like me to open the window?
I should like you to type these letters at once, please.

Want sometimes means *need*.

He'll want a lot of new clothes next year.
You want a new hat.
You won't want all that money.
How much time will you want?
This house wants a coat of paint.
Your suit wants cleaning.
He's very tired. He wants a holiday.

(c) *Wish* means to desire or hope for something not likely to happen. *Wish* is often used for *want* in more formal speech or writing:

I wish (that) I could afford a new car. (But I can't)

I wish (that) you would work harder. (But you won't)

Girls often wish (that) they were boys. (But they're not)

I wish (that) the summer would soon come. (But it's still winter)

He wishes (that) he had more money. (But he hasn't)

I wish I could find my pen.

I wish you wouldn't talk so loudly.

Do you wish you were as clever as Tom?

Susan wishes she had finished her work.

I wish to speak to Mr Brown, please.

If you wish to learn English you must work hard.

I don't wish to see you again.

How much do you wish to spend?

If you wish, you may stay here for the night.

He does not wish me to tell you his name.

NEW WORDS

address (ə'dres)

camping ('kampiŋ)

carriage ('karidʒ)

firm (fəːm)

fisherman ('fiʃəmən)

fun (fʌn)

information (infə'meiʃn)

Messrs ('mesəz)

parcel ('paːsl)

park (paːk)

relation (ri'leiʃn)

sale (seil)

share (ʃeə)

speech (spiːtʃ)

speed (spiːd)

tent (tent)

wedding ('wediŋ)

advertise, advertised ('advətaiz, 'advətaizd)

agree, agreed (ə'griː, ə'griːd)

argue, argued ('aːgjuː, 'aːgjuːd)

blame, blamed (bleim, bleimd)

dine, dined (dain, daind)

enclose, enclosed (ən'klouz, ən'klouzd)

hide, hid, hidden (haid, hid, hidn)

quarrel, quarrelled ('kworl, 'kworld)

receive, received (ri'siːv, ri'siːvd)

recommend, recommended ('rekə'mend, 'rekə'mendid)

remind, reminded (ri'maind, ri'maindid)

rush, rushed (rʌʃ, rʌʃt)

suppose, supposed (sə'pouz, sə'pouzd)

save, saved (seiv, seivd)

uncork, uncorked (ʌn'koːk, ʌn'koːkt)

wish, wished (wiʃ, wiʃt)

afterwards ('aːftəwədz)

amusing (ə'mjuːziŋ)

eighteenth ('ei'tiːnθ)

excellent ('eksələnt)

faithfully ('feiθfəli)

hardly ('haːdli)

indeed (in'diːd)

limited (Ltd) ('limitid)

poor (puə, poː)

satisfactory ('satis'faktri)

seldom ('seldəm)

usual ('juːʒuəl)

Idioms

to grow up (tə 'grou 'ʌp)

when a birthday comes round (wen ə 'bəːθdei 'kʌmz 'raund)

to drink someone's health (tə 'driŋk 'sʌmwʌnz 'helθ)

Many happy returns of the day! ('meni 'hapi ri'təːnz əv ðə 'dei)

it seemed a pity to (it 'siːmd ə 'piti tə)

quite a lot ('kwait ə 'lot)

to be all smiles (tə bi 'oːl 'smailz)

to dine out (tə 'dain 'aut)

Let me tell you . . . ('let mi 'tel 'juː)

Cheers! (tʃiəz)

to make a speech (tə 'meik ə 'spiːtʃ)

that reminds me ('ðat ri'maindz mi)

just round the corner ('dʒʌst 'raund ðə 'koːnə)

to make fun of (tə 'meik 'fʌn əv)

EXERCISES

A. *Dictation*

Mr Brown looked through the window of the train as he travelled northward to Edinburgh. He saw that the fields were green, the hedges were tidy and the animals looked fat and well. He thought that England was a pleasant country to live in—a country where you could go anywhere you liked and say what you liked.

The wheels of the train rolled on and on. Mr Brown had got up early that morning. He had washed and shaved and dressed and had had his breakfast before half past seven, and now he was feeling tired . . . Slowly his eyes closed, and he was asleep . . .

He woke up suddenly. Through the window, quite close to the train, was the sea—the grey North Sea with a grey sky above it. He knew that he was now in Scotland and that it would not be long before he was in Edinburgh.

B. *Answer these questions in sentences:*

1. Why did the Browns go out to dinner that evening?
2. What did Susan buy David for a present?
3. Why will David need a lot of new clothes soon?
4. How did Mr Brown know about the restaurant where they had dinner?
5. Why did they drink David's health?
6. What do the English call coffee (*a*) without milk, (*b*) with milk?
7. Why didn't they want a taxi from the restaurant to the theatre?
8. What wine do you like best?
9. On what day is your birthday?
10. How many brothers or sisters have you, and what are their names?

C. *Put* much *or* many *into these sentences:*

1. There weren't . . . people in the park.
2. She has . . . friends in England.
3. How . . . money have you?
4. Have you read . . . books this year.
5. Have you had . . . rain this summer?
6. Are there . . . students in your class?
7. How . . . chairs are there in this room?
8. There isn't . . . milk in this tea.
9. We haven't . . . coffee.
10. You have made too . . . mistakes in your exercise.

D. *Put the verbs* want, like *or* wish *into these sentences:*

1. I . . . I had a new bicycle.
2. Mrs Brown . . . some new curtains in the sitting-room.
3. David . . . oranges, but he doesn't . . . onions.
4. Do you . . . me to type these letters now, Mr Robinson?
5. We don't . . . to go to the same place for our holidays this year.
6. He doesn't . . . much sugar in his tea.
7. Susan sometimes . . . she lived in London.
8. Now that they have three children they . . . a new house.
9. Would you . . . to look round the factory?
10. How much money do you . . .?

E. *Make each of these sentences negative in two different ways:*

1. He is a friend of mine.
2. They have been here before.
3. Tom is a clever young man.
4. Mr Brown is going to London tomorrow.
5. I had met him before.
6. She will be here before tea-time.
7. It has been a fine day today.
8. I'll go to school this afternoon.
9. They are living at Bishopton now.
10. David is going to Oxford in October.

F. *Imagine that you have seen in a newspaper an advertisement for something you wish to buy. Write a letter sending your order to the advertiser.*

G. *Write a paragraph or two about the ways in which food in your own country is different from food in England.*

H. *Write a paragraph about birthdays in your own country.*

I. *Make questions from these sentences:*
   1. He can swim very well.
   2. We must drive carefully in the town.
   3. He needs a new hat.
   4. He has an egg for breakfast every morning.
   5. He does his homework each evening.
   6. The Browns have a large garden.
   7. He dared me to jump off the bridge.
   8. Tom should talk more quietly in the theatre.
   9. They may go home now.
   10. Mr Brown will be in London tomorrow.

J. *Use the following special verbs in (a) affirmative sentences, (b) negative sentences, (c) interrogative sentences:*

   are; has; did; shall; will; may; can; ought; must; need; dare.

K. *Add question-tags to these sentences:*
   1. David will soon go to university.
   2. Tom can't go to the theatre this evening.
   3. Mr Brown went to Edinburgh last week.
   4. Mrs Brown goes shopping on Monday morning.
   5. That driver ought to be more careful.
   6. David needn't work so hard this year.
   7. We shan't be at home this evening.
   8. Mr Brown walked to the station this morning.
   9. It'll be late before we get home.
   10. Mrs Brown has a lot of friends in Bishopton.

L. *Put a pronoun into the blank space in each of these sentences:*

1. I gave the book to . . .
2. He asked . . . a question.
3. We told . . . what had happened.
4. I have bought a new dress for . . .
5. The dog was hungry so I gave . . . some dinner.
6. The train was very full but the porter found . . . a seat.
7. She said the chair was hard so he brought . . . a cushion.
8. "Get . . . a book from that shelf, please."
9. He told . . . the banks were closed so I lent . . . some money.
10. They were lost so we showed . . . the way.

M. *Put these sentences into the passive:*

1. Buses take the workers home in the evening.
2. They make cars and bicycles in Birmingham.
3. Someone left the light on all night.
4. They opened a new cinema in Bishopton last week.
5. People will invite you to their homes.
6. They will paint this bicycle red.
7. Someone has washed these curtains since last Monday.
8. They have taken the butter and eggs to the market.
9. They were cleaning all the carpets.
10. Someone was selling all the houses in the street.

N. *Put the given adverb into the right place in these sentences:*

1. We go abroad for our holidays (*always*).
2. I have finished my work (*almost*).
3. Susan gets home by half past five (*usually*).
4. Tom has bought a new car (*just*).
5. I have been to England before (*never*).
6. People catch cold in winter (*often*).
7. Susan goes shopping in London (*sometimes*).
8. Mr Brown travels to London by train (*usually*).
9. He walks to the station (*seldom*).
10. The train had started when they served dinner (*hardly*).

O. *Write ten sentences, each using the name of an article of clothing.*

P. *Put the correct form of the verb into these sentences:*

1. If it is fine Mr Brown (*walk*) to the station.
2. If he had enough money Tom (*buy*) a new car.
3. While Mrs Brown (*wait*) for the bus yesterday she (*meet*) a friend.
4. Cars (*make*) in this country and many (*sell*) abroad.
5. On most days Mr Brown (*walk*) to the station, but today he (*go*) by bus.
6. Susan (*be*) at the office since nine o'clock and at five she (*go*) home.
7. I (*come*) to England three weeks ago and I (*stay*) until next Thursday.
8. We (*go*) into the country every week-end if it (*be*) fine.
9. She (*go*) for a walk after she (*finish*) her work.
10. You (*go*) home, children, if you (*finish*) your exercise.

Q. *The Conversation passage tells how the Brown family spent the evening of David's birthday. Write a composition on* The Browns' Evening Out.

This Man Shakespeare

There is a story about a film director in the early days of Hollywood who saw a Shakespeare play at the theatre and thought it would make a good film. After the performance he said to his manager, "Who is this man Shakespeare? Why isn't he writing for *us*? I want to see him. Get him on the telephone in the morning."

director (diˈrektə)

LESSON 11

The Browns Go to the Races

PEOPLE often ask, "What is Britain's national sport?" Is it cricket? or football? or boxing perhaps? Who can say? But if anyone asked that question one hundred and fifty years ago, it was easy to give the answer; the national sports were those in which horses took part—hunting, riding and racing.

Few people can afford to hunt today, but even if they have not a horse of their own many people enjoy horse-riding, and watching horse-jumping (or 'show jumping' as it is called), especially on television. But the most popular sport with horses is still horse-racing. There are race-courses in most parts of England and race-meetings are held in spring, summer and autumn. The first big meeting is at Lincoln in March and the last is at Manchester in November.

Some people go to the races to see the horses and to enjoy themselves, but others are more interested in betting. And even if a man cannot go to the races himself, he can still place a bet on a horse he thinks will win.

The most famous race in the year is the Derby, which is run at Epsom usually on the first Wednesday in June. The race-course at Epsom stands high on the Downs, not far from London, and during Derby week it is filled by a large crowd of people, rich and poor, young and old, who have come there to enjoy themselves and perhaps win some money on a lucky bet.

Susan and David had never been to the Derby, so this year Mr Brown decided to take the whole family. He knew the roads would be crowded, so they set off early, taking their picnic lunch with them. But they found that all the roads out of London to Epsom were full of cars, motor-coaches, motor-cycles, bicycles and even horses and carts. All the world seemed to be going to the races, and everyone wanted to get there too fast for safety.

Epsom Downs on Derby Day is something that no one can every forget. There is nothing else like it in the world. For thousands of Londoners Derby Day is not only a race-meeting: it is one of the great days in the year, an outing for the whole family. They come there by car, by train, by bus—somehow. They bring their food with them, and all round the race-course you can see family parties sitting on the grass or in their cars eating and shouting and laughing and enjoying themselves.

There is plenty to do as well as watching the racing itself. A huge fair is set up on the Downs, with swings and other games for children—and older people, too. Men walk about selling toys, balloons, ice-cream, sweets—anything that they think people will buy. And everywhere there are bookmakers (*bookies*, they are called) and their clerks taking bets from the crowd.

The big race is usually at 3.20 p.m. and then everyone pushes to the rail round the course to watch the race. For a few minutes the noise stops: the bookies and the ice-cream sellers and the men with the swings stop shouting. All eyes watch the line of brown and black and grey horses, with their riders in brightly-coloured coats and caps, as they race down the narrow path of green grass between the crowds. In this greatest race of the year it is each man for himself.

When the race is over and the owner has led in the winner, the noise and the shouting start again. As soon as the racing finishes at the end of the afternoon, the motor-coaches and cars and motor-cycles and bicycles begin the long, slow journey back to London. Derby Day is over for another year.

CONVERSATION

(*On the road between London and Epsom*)

MRS BROWN: What a crowd! I don't think I've ever seen so
many cars on the road. And the noise! I can hardly
hear myself speak.

MR BROWN: It isn't the cars that worry me. Even if you have
to go slowly, the cars keep in a line one behind the other.
It's the motor-cycles and bicycles that make the trouble.
They're not safe. They go in and out among the cars
and you never know when you're going to hit one. It
doesn't matter how careful you are yourself. . . . Look
out, there! Did you see that silly boy on the motor-
cycle with the girl behind him? I nearly hit him. Driving
in this crowd isn't easy.

SUSAN: Perhaps we ought to have come by train after all.

MR BROWN: No, we'll soon be there now. It's a good way
from the station to the course, and there's always a big
crowd waiting for the trains after the races. You get
away more quickly if you have a car of your own. Ah,
we're coming on to the course now. We'll leave the car,
then we'll find a good place to have lunch. We'll go to
the stands before the big race, but it's more fun out on
the Downs if you've never been here before on Derby
Day.

• • • •

(*In the stand before the big race*)

MRS BROWN: We can see very well from here.

MR BROWN: The horses are lined up ready to start. 'Under
starter's orders' they call it. There they go! They're off!
We'll each watch our own horse.

DAVID: Peterkin is off to a good start with Morning Star just behind him. Come on, Peterkin! I've got fifty pence on you.

SUSAN: Which you borrowed from me. Where's Pretty Polly? Oh, I can't see her.

MR BROWN: Her rider's wearing yellow and blue. There she is—fourth—no fifth, I think.

MRS BROWN: Quick, John. Lend me the glasses! Don't the colours look lovely against the green grass?

DAVID: Oh, Mother, who cares about the colours? Where's Peterkin?—that's what I want to know. Give me the glasses, please.

MR BROWN: Peterkin's still in front, isn't he?

DAVID: Yes, but Morning Star's close to him. And Pretty Polly's coming up. She's third now, Susan.

SUSAN: Oh, let me look. So she is. Pretty Polly. Pretty Polly —oh run!

MR BROWN: Now they're turning into the straight. We shall see them without the glasses soon.

DAVID: Here they come. What's happened to Peterkin? Morning Star's passed him.

SUSAN: So has Pretty Polly. And she's going to pass Morning Star, too. She's going to win. She is! She is!

MR BROWN: I think she is, Susan. How much have you on her?

SUSAN: A pound. At five to one. Oh, Pretty Polly, come *on*! She's passed him. She's passed Morning Star—she's going to win. She's won! Hooray!

DAVID: And you've won five pounds. With your own pound, that makes six. Oh dear, what a pity I've had my birthday!

MRS BROWN: Well, Susan, that must be what is called 'beginner's luck'. Come on, we'll get the money you've won. And I think we could all do with a drink after that. I know I could.

SENTENCE PATTERNS

42.   Verbs not used in the Present Continuous

There are some verbs which are seldom found in the Present Continuous. The feelings or states they describe are not under the control of the persons about whom they are used, nor are they thought of as having a beginning or an end. In the following examples we should expect the verbs in italics to be in the Present Continuous but the Simple Present is used instead.

You are telling me the truth, and I *believe* you.
I *don't know* what is happening, and I *don't care*.
She is being unkind to me, but I *forgive* her.
I *forget* the name of the man who is talking to Mary.

Do you *hear* what he is saying?
I am leaving the party because I *hate* these people.
I *like* these people, so I'm enjoying myself.
I *notice* you are wearing a new coat.
I *see* the Bishopton team is playing at home this week.
He *wants* to speak to Susan, but she is walking away.

Other verbs which seldom appear in the Present Continuous are: *mean, possess, recognise, refuse, remember, seem, suppose, smell, understand, wish*. These verbs are sometimes called Non-conclusive verbs.

43.   *Own*

(*a*) Each boy had his own book.
   Get on with your own work.
   One usually prefers to sleep in one's own bed.
   Most countries have their own language.
   Even his own brother would not speak to him.
   Mrs Brown usually gets her own way.

(*b*) One day Susan will have a home of her own.
   Each child was given a desk of his own.
   I wish I had a room of my own.
   You can learn to drive a friend's car, but it is better to have
     a car of your own.
   She doesn't need any flowers: she has a garden of her own.

44.   *Too—Enough*

(*a*) *Too* = also, as well

   In speech we use *too* more often than *also*.

   Have you been to the party, too?
   You, too, must come with us.
   I saw my aunt at the station, too.
   Is he coming, too?

Do you live in Bishopton, too?
Aren't you going, too?
This, too, is very important.
Are these your children, too?
There are some people, too, who enjoy show jumping.

As well is often used for *too*.

David is coming as well.
I'll take you with us as well.
There's room for the children as well.
I'm afraid we can't take the dog as well.
We have been to Edinburgh, and to Cardiff as well.

(b) *Too* = too much, too little

She was too tired to walk to the station.
We are too late to catch the train now.
He is too young to go to the university.
He is too lazy to work hard.
You are too old to run for the bus.
It is too far to walk.
You have done too little work today.
It is too early for dinner.
He drives too fast for safety.
He paid too much for that pen.
There are too many people here.
You have put too much sugar in my tea.
He works too slowly.
You can't be too careful.
This house is too small for us.

(c) *Enough* = sufficient
Enough comes before a noun, but follows an adjective.

Have you enough money?
There isn't enough room to sit down.
Have we enough time to buy some cigarettes?
Have you enough sugar in your coffee?

I have enough children; I don't want any more.
He is clever enough to pass his examination.
It is easy enough to make money.

NEW WORDS

balloon (bə'luːn)
bet (bet)
　betting ('betiŋ)
bookie ('buki)
　bookmaker ('bukmeikə)
boxing ('boksiŋ)
cap (kap)
cart (kaːt)
difficulty ('difiklti)
fair (feə)
horse (hoːs)
line (lain)
meeting ('miːtiŋ)
motor-coach ('moutə'koutʃ)
outing ('autiŋ)
owner ('ounə)
path (paːθ)
race (reis)
　racing ('reisiŋ)
　race-course ('reiskoːs)
rail (reil)

rule (ruːl)
safety ('seifti)
stand (stand)
swing (swiŋ)
winner ('winə)

borrow, borrowed ('borou, 'boroud)
hate, hated (heit, 'heitid)
hunt, hunted (hʌnt, 'hʌntid)
push, pushed (puʃ, puʃt)

hooray! (hu'rei)
huge (hjuːdʒ)
itself (it'self)
lazy ('leizi)
oneself (wʌn'self)
popular ('popjulə)
rich (ritʃ)
safe (seif)
somehow ('sʌmhau)

Idioms

to place a bet (tə 'pleis ə 'bet)
each man for himself ('iːtʃ 'man fə him'self)
I can't hear myself speak (ai 'kaːnt 'hiə miself 'spiːk)
Look out! ('luk 'aut)
it's a good way from . . . (its ə 'gud 'wei frəm)
They're off! ('ðei ər 'of)
off to a good start ('of tu ə 'gud 'staːt)

EXERCISES

A. *Answer the following questions in sentences:*

1. What is the national sport in your own country?
2. What is 'the Derby'?
3. Where and when is it run?
4. How can you tell the owner of each horse?
5. What else can be seen at Epsom besides the racing?
6. Which horse won the race?
7. How much did Susan win?
8. Why did Mr Brown take the whole family to the Derby?
9. What do we call the people who take bets on a race-course?
10. What would happen if Mr Brown did not drive carefully?

B. *Put the* -self *pronouns into these sentences:*

1. She hurt when she fell down the stairs (*herself*).
2. I decided to do the work (*myself*).
3. He cut while he was shaving (*himself*).
4. The Queen will be at the concert (*herself*).
5. If you can't do the work you must find someone who can (*yourself*).
6. We like the house, but we don't like the town in which it it is built (*itself*).
7. I often ask why I don't go back to my own country (*myself*).
8. I haven't read the book, but my friend says it is very good (*myself*).
9. One can lose quite easily in this large town (*oneself*).
10. She shut in her room all day (*herself*).

C. *Rewrite these sentences, using* enough *instead of* too:

You arrived too late to catch the bus.
You did not arrive early enough to catch the bus.

1. It was too dark to see where we were going.

2. This house is too small for our family.
3. This exercise is too hard for you.
4. It is too cold to go out without a coat.
5. Mrs Brown is too short to reach that high shelf.
6. Your shoes are too dirty to come into the house.
7. Mr Brown thinks Susan is too young to get married.

D. *Rewrite these sentences, using the verb* may. *Add the word* permission *or* possibility *in brackets after each sentence:*

1. Will you let me see your garden, please?
2. Perhaps he will arrive on the next train.
3. Possibly he is in London today.
4. Will you please allow them to leave early?
5. Please will you let us come in?
6. Mrs Brown will perhaps send for the doctor if David isn't better.
7. Will you allow me to open the window?
8. I shall perhaps decide to spend the summer in Switzerland.
9. Will you let me carry your bag for you?
10. It will rain tomorrow perhaps.

E. *Put prepositions into these sentences:*

1. I met her while I was . . . holiday.
2. She fell . . . the stairs.
3. I was sitting . . . him in the bus.
4. She will arrive . . . lunch.
5. February comes . . . January and March.
6. She went . . . her friends . . . the seaside.
7. She spent a lot of money . . . presents . . . her friends.
8. He looked . . . the letter, and then gave it . . . his sister.
9. There has been a lot of rain . . . the day.
10. As he was playing . . . the stream the boy fell . . . the water.

F. *The following are reported statements and questions. Give the words the speaker used:*

1. He said he was going to London the next day.
2. He asked Mary where she was going.
3. She told me she had been to the Derby.
4. He said he thought it would rain the next day.
5. They said they didn't know why the train was late.
6. She told us she couldn't read English very well.
7. The teacher said his students worked hard but he didn't think they would pass the examination.
8. Mrs Brown asked if there was anything good on television.
9. The doctor wanted to know how long David had been ill.
10. Mr Brown asked David if he had finished his homework.

G. *Describe a sporting event that you have seen.*

H. *Write a paragraph giving advice to a person driving a car on a busy road.*

I. *In the Conversation the Browns are talking about the race they are watching. Write a paragraph describing the race as they saw it.*

J. *Finish these sentences with a time clause:*

1. The Browns will go home when . . .
2. Everyone was very excited while . . .
3. You should not talk in the theatre after . . .
4. Wait here until . . .
5. They got out of the train as soon as . . .
6. You may stay with me as long as . . .
7. No sooner had we set off than . . .
8. When . . . we'll all go to the cinema.
9. After . . . the race-course was quite empty.
10. While . . . we enjoyed ourselves very much.

K. *Add question-tags to these sentences:*

1. You are a bad boy, . . .?
2. I'm one of your friends, . . .?
3. We used to go abroad for our holidays, . . .?
4. We ought to go home now, . . .?
5. You're not staying for tea, . . .?
6. We shan't stay for more than an hour, . . .?
7. He may go home now, . . .?
8. He works at the bicycle factory, . . .?
9. They got home before midnight, . . .?
10. You did your homework last night, . . .?

L. *Put the verbs in these sentences into the right tense: Present Continuous, Present Perfect, Past or Future.*

1. I (*be*) here since last June.
2. We (*live*) in Bishopton since 1947.
3. When he (*finish*) his work he (*go*) home.
4. They (*arrive*) on the race-course at 1 o'clock.
5. She (*do*) her shopping and now she (*wait*) for a bus.
6. David (*read*) the book he (*receive*) as a birthday present.
7. I (*work*) hard all the week and now I (*rest*).
8. I (*not enjoy*) this film because I (*see*) it before.
9. Mr Brown (*visit*) many countries during the past ten years.
10. Tom (*live*) in London when he (*be*) a boy.

M. *Put the verb* shall, will, should, *or* would *into each of these sentences:*

1. I think you . . . be more careful.
2. I . . . go to the Derby, if it is fine.
3. He . . . earn more money if he worked harder.
4. . . . you be in London next week?
5. The doctor . . . be here before three o'clock.
6. He . . . like to spend a holiday in Wales.
7. David . . . do his homework before he starts to play cards.

8. I hope this horse . . . win.
9. He knew his horse . . . win.
10. We . . . drive better if we took driving lessons.

N. *Put the word* too *or* enough *into these sentences:*

1. We should like to come to the races.
2. It was late to cook a hot meal.
3. This bag is light to carry in your hand.
4. I have money to pay my own fare.
5. There is much noise in this room.
6. It is early to go to bed.
7. He is old to look after himself.
8. We'll arrange a picnic if people want to go.
9. He is old to go back to school.
10. Is this book yours?

O. *Write twelve sentences, each about one of the twelve months of the year.*

P. *Put the correct form of the verb* talk, speak, say, *or* tell *into the blank spaces in these sentences:*

1. She dislikes him so much she won't even . . . to him.
2. She . . . me what had happened when I met her last week.
3. The woman . . . all the afternoon, but her husband didn't . . . a word.
4. Who . . . you the name of the people who live next door?
5. "I . . . you so," she . . .
6. Never . . . to me about it again.
7. Can you . . . me the way to the station, please?
8. He stood in the street . . . with some friends.
9. He cannot . . . a word of English.
10. Did she . . . how long she would be?

Q. *Write down the Past Tense and Past Participle of these verbs:*
see; break; fall; cut; sleep; give; swim; ring; sit; show.

R. *Put the word* much, more, many, less, *or* fewer *into these sentences:*

1. How . . . money have you in the bank?
2. You will have . . . difficulty with your exercises if you work . . . in class.
3. There is plenty of room on the train; there are . . . people than I expected.
4. . . . people in England today have cars.
5. I don't like so . . . sugar in my tea; please put . . . in next time.
6. We haven't . . . friends in this country.
7. There are . . . poor people in England than there were fifty years ago.
8. Hurry up. We haven't . . . time.
9. . . . people live in London than in Birmingham.
10. . . . hands make light work.

Rule of the Road

Our rule of the road is difficult quite,
As you're riding or driving along.
If you keep to your left you are sure to be right;
If you keep to your right you'll be wrong.

LESSON 12

Susan Gets Engaged

SUSAN BROWN and Tom Smith first met at a Christmas party at a friend's house. He was then a student at a university and she had just left school. That was more than two years ago. During this time they have become very close friends, and now they are engaged to be married.

Tom is a very nice boy—and Susan loves him very much. He is clever, too. He did well at the university and now he has a good job at a cycle factory near Bishopton, where he is making excellent progress. Learning to be a manager is interesting work and Tom enjoys it. Although he is not earning a very large salary at the moment, he hopes to be a manager himself soon. Susan's father and mother like Tom and are glad that their daughter has found someone who will look after her and be kind to her. So when Susan and Tom told them that they wanted to get engaged, Mr and Mrs Brown were very happy.

The young people have not made any arrangements for the wedding yet. Getting married is very expensive, and they will have to save some money first, so they do not mind if they have to put off the wedding for a little while. They will want to find a house, too, and this is not easy. Many young married people today live with the boy's or with the girl's family, but it is better for them to have a house of their own. So Tom and Susan will have to work hard, save as much money as they can and look for a house before they can get married. But as Tom is only twenty-two and Susan is only twenty, this does not matter very much.

Susan is very proud of her engagement ring. Buying an engagement ring is a serious matter: it is something that does not happen often, so they spent a day in London together for the event. They looked in many jewellers' windows before Susan made up her mind. At last they saw what they wanted in a shop in Regent Street. But they did not buy it at once; no woman ever does that! The assistant brought out tray after tray of rings, some of them very expensive. Susan enjoyed trying on rings costing many hundreds of pounds and comparing one with another, even though she knew that she and Tom could not afford them. At last, she asked for the diamond ring in the window which she and Tom had liked, and this was the ring they bought.

When Susan got to the office the next morning, all the girls at once noticed the ring on the third finger of her left hand, and said how pleased they were. But Mr Robinson, the manager, to whom Susan is secretary, did not notice it for three days, and he only noticed it then because Susan waved it in front of his eyes. Susan thought that her brother David would make fun of her when he saw the ring, but to her surprise he kissed her and said "Very nice too!" Susan was so pleased, she nearly cried.

When Mr Carter, the manager of Tom's factory, heard that Tom and Susan were engaged, he sent for him and told him he was going to ask the directors to raise his salary. "You'll need it when you're married, as you'll very soon find out," he said.

CONVERSATION

MR BROWN: So they're getting engaged.

MRS BROWN: Yes. They seem very happy about it.

MR BROWN: Do you mind? Aren't they both rather young?

MRS BROWN: Oh, I don't know. Susan's nearly twenty-one and Tom's twenty-two. After all, they don't want to get married straight away.

MR BROWN: Yes, I suppose it's all right. I can't get used to the idea that Susan's grown up though. I still think of her as a girl. It seems to me only yesterday that she was a school-girl running about in short skirts.

MRS BROWN: It seems to me only yesterday that she was a small baby learning to walk. But we must get it into our minds that both the children are growing up. And Tom's a very nice boy. I'm very fond of him.

MR BROWN: Yes, I think so, too. He's honest and kind and he works hard. I was talking to Carter, his manager, the other day. He says Tom is going to do well. He has a good brain, he knows his job and he gets on well with the workers. Carter says he'll make an excellent manager when he's had a few years' experience.

Mrs Brown: They seem very much in love. And that's the thing that really matters.

Mr Brown: When are they thinking of getting married?

Mrs Brown: I don't think they've made any plans. They certainly haven't any date in mind yet.

Mr Brown: Finding a house is going to be the most difficult matter. It costs so much to buy or to build a house at the present time. They could live here to start with though.

Mrs Brown: No. They must have a house of their own. Young people ought to make a new start in their own home. Living with relations is not a good idea. Can the Bank help?

Mr Brown: I'll talk to Tom about it and see what I can do. That's a nice ring he bought her.

Mrs Brown: Yes. Susan has very good taste, I must say.

Mr Brown: She gets that from you, my dear. Look what a good husband you chose!

Mrs Brown: Well, dear, if Susan gets as good a husband as I did, we shall not have anything to worry about.

Mr Brown: And if Susan is as good a wife as her mother, Tom'll be a lucky boy. Now please do you mind if I have my supper?

SENTENCE PATTERNS

45.   Adverbial Clauses

Time—Condition—Reason—Concession

Time

He came home as soon as he had finished his work.
He visited the National Gallery when he was in London.
I'll cook the lunch while you are at church.
Bring the chairs from the garden before it starts to rain.
He spoke to the actors after the play was over.

Condition

You may go home if you have finished your work.
If it is fine tomorrow we shall go to the seaside.
I'll visit his house if I am in London next week.
I should go to bed early if I were you.
If people eat too much they get fat.

Reason

We stayed at home because it was raining.
As you are here, you can help us with the work.
She bought a new hat because she was going to a party.
David went to bed as he wasn't feeling well.
Because he is getting married, the manager gave him a higher
   salary.

Concession: although, though

She can read without glasses, although she is over seventy.
He has passed all his examinations, although he is quite young.
I haven't finished yet, although I've been working all day.
It is very warm today, although it is still winter.
Although they haven't a house yet, Susan and Tom are getting
   married next year.
Although the Thompsons live in the town, they often spend a
   holiday in the country.
Although they had very little money, they were very happy.
Mr Thompson is over seventy; he is still working though.
Tom has bought a new car; he hasn't paid for it yet though.
We haven't any money left; we had a good holiday though.
They work hard all the week; they enjoy themselves at the week-
   end though.

46.   *Mind—Matter*

Mind

(*a*) Noun = the part of us we think with.
   He has a very clear mind.

We must keep this in mind.
She hasn't made up her mind yet.
The poor man is out of his mind.
He has a number of new ideas in mind.
Can you hold all this in your mind at once?

(b) Verb = to be important to, to be concerned about, to object.

Do you mind if I close the window?
Do you mind passing me that newspaper?
They don't mind what you do in their house.
Will she mind if we don't stay to tea?
Will you have a cigarette? I don't mind if I do.
You mustn't mind if they have to leave early.
Never mind the crowd; we shall soon get there.
Have you lost your money? Never mind: I'll give you some
    more.

(c) Verb = to look after, take care of, be careful.

Mind you don't fall downstairs.
She will mind the house while we are out.
Mind the step!
Someone must stay at home to mind the baby.
In a London Underground station the porters shout, "Mind
    the doors!" when the train is ready to start.
It is not polite to say to someone "Mind your own business!"

Matter

(a) Noun = affair, happening.

This is an important matter.
We must think carefully about this matter.
This is a matter for the police.
The matter we are talking about is quite different.
This is no laughing matter.
There are two or three matters I want to see you about.

(*b*) Noun = trouble, wrong.

> What is the matter?
> What's the matter with Tom? Is he ill?
> There's something the matter with this car.
> Is there anything the matter?
> Is anything the matter?
> There's nothing the matter with this hotel. It's one of the best in London.
> I don't know what's the matter with him.

(*c*) Verb = be important (Note *matter* here is more impersonal than *mind*).

> Does it matter?
> Does it matter if he is late?
> Does it matter to you if we don't come?
> Don't worry; it doesn't matter.
> Nothing matters, so long as you're happy.
> It doesn't matter to me whether he goes or stays.

47.   *Not any—No*

There are *not* (aren't) *any* flowers in our garden.
There are *no* flowers in our garden.

There are *not* (aren't) *any* knives on the table.
There are *no* knives on the table.

There is *not* (isn't) *any* sugar in my coffee.
There is (there's) *no* sugar in my coffee.

There is *not* (isn't) *any* milk in his tea.
There is (there's) *no* milk in his tea.

She has *not* (hasn't) *any* friends.
She has *no* friends.

We have *not* (haven't) *any* vegetables in our garden.
We have *no* vegetables in our garden.

David has *not* (hasn't) *any* money.
David has *no* money.

48.   Interrogatives

Who?   What?   Which?

Who? is used for persons in general, and is always a pronoun.

Who lives in this house?
Who would like another cup of tea?
Who is (Who's) going home?
Who will (Who'll) come with me?
Who broke that window?

Although interrogative *Whom?* is still used in written English as
the objective form, *Who?* is almost always used in spoken English
for both subject and object.
The possessive form is *Whose?*

Who (whom) did you meet at the party?
Who (whom) have you invited to dinner?
Who (whom) have you given the book to?
Who (whom) do you buy your milk from?
Whose house is that?
Whose car did you ride in?
Whose coat are you wearing?

What? is used as a pronoun for things in general, and as an adjective for people and things in general. The same form is used for
subject and object, and there is no possessive form.

(*a*) Pronoun   What is happening?
                 What are you doing?
                 What is that on the table?

What do you want?
What can I do for you?
What are you talking about?
What is it made of?
What did you open it with?

(b) Adjective What time is it?
What language does he speak?
What pictures hang on the wall?
What friends did you meet?
What servants will you need?
What train are you going by?
What books did he tell you about?
What countries do they come from?

Which? is used as a pronoun or adjective to pick out one or more persons or things from a limited number. The same form is used for subject and object, and there is no possessive form.

Which is your brother? (There aren't many to choose from)
Which girl do you like best?
Which hat is yours?
Which book will you have?
Which is your favourite game?
Which is the London train?
Which is Mr Brown, please?
Which way do we go?

Notice that where *Who? What?* or *Which?* is not the subject, there is inversion of subject and verb.

Who did you see?
Whose coat has she taken?
What have you done?
Which book did he choose?

NEW WORDS

brain (brein)
date (deit)
diamond (ˈdaiəmənd)
experience (iksˈpiəriəns)
finger (ˈfiŋgə)
jeweller (ˈdʒuːələ)
progress (ˈprougres)
ring (riŋ)
salary (ˈsaləri)
sum (sʌm)
taste (teist)

compare, compared (kəmˈpeə, kəmˈpeəd)

cry, cried (krai, kraid)
kiss, kissed (kis, kist)
marry, married (ˈmari, ˈmarid)
notice, noticed (ˈnoutis, ˈnoutist)
raise, raised (reiz, reizd)

although (ɔːlðou)
engaged (inˈgeidʒd)
honest (ˈonist)
kind (kaind)
underground (ˈʌndəˈgraund)

Idioms

to get engaged (tə ˈget inˈgeidʒd)
a house of your own (ə ˈhaus əv jər ˈoun)
Oh, I don't know (ˈou ai ˈdount ˈnou)
it seems only yesterday that . . . (it ˈsiːmz ounli ˈjestədi ðət)
to get it into one's mind (head) (tə ˈget it intə wʌnz ˈmaind)
to get on well with (tə ˈget on ˈwel wið)
to be in love (tə ˈbi in ˈlʌv)
to have good taste (tə hav ˈgud ˈteist)
to make good progress (tə meik ˈgud ˈprougres)

EXERCISES

A. *Answer these questions in sentences:*

1. What does Tom Smith do for a living?
2. Why were Mr and Mrs Brown pleased when Susan got engaged?
3. What did Tom buy Susan on their visit to London?

4. Why didn't Mr Robinson notice the ring on Susan's finger?

5. What did Susan think David would do when he heard she was engaged?

6. What did Mr Carter, the manager, do when Tom got engaged?

7. What does Mr Carter think of him?

8. Why do Susan and Tom want a house of their own?

9. On which finger does an Englishwoman wear an engagement ring?

10. How much older is Tom than Susan?

B. *Put the word* mind *or* matter *into these sentences:*

1. He doesn't . . . what we do.

2. Do you . . . if I smoke a cigarette?

3. Do you know what is the . . . with Susan?

4. . . . you don't fall!

5. He made up his . . . to have a holiday in Switzerland.

6. It doesn't . . . to me what you do with your money.

7. We have left him at home to . . . the baby.

8. Why has she gone home? Is there anything the . . .?

9. The . . . they are talking about is very important.

10. Can you keep all these things in . . . at once?

C. *Complete each of these sentences with an adverbial clause of the kind asked for:*

1. They had a house in London (*time*) . . .

2. We shan't go to the races (*condition*) . . .

3. They set off for London (*concession*) . . .

4. The Browns are going out to dinner this evening (*reason*) . . .

5. David often goes to the cinema (*time*) . . .

6. I should be very careful (*condition*) . . .

7. Mrs Brown is tired (*reason*) . . .

8. Mrs Brown is not tired (*concession*) . . .

9. Mr Brown was reading a newspaper (*time*) . . .

10. They live in London (*reason*) . . .

D. *Use each of these phrases in a sentence:*

make up one's mind; it seems only yesterday; quite a lot; just round the corner; find fault with; it's hard to say; go for a walk; make an early start.

E. *Write a composition on* A person I admire.

F. *Add the correct question word to these sentences:*

1. . . . of the two boys is your brother?
2. . . . are you doing today?
3. Someone has left his hat. . . . is it?
4. . . . did you travel with?
5. . . . hands are the cleanest?
6. . . . boy were you speaking to?
7. . . . is the matter with John?
8. . . . picture do you like best?
9. . . . do you like best for breakfast?
10. . . . gave you those cigarettes?

G. *Use each of the following words in a separate sentence:*

experience; salary; popular; safety; seldom; parcel; hardly; believe; splendid; determined.

H. *Give the correct form of the Present Tense in these sentences:*

1. I (*get up*) at seven o'clock every morning.
2. John (*talk*) to a friend outside his house.
3. I (*forget*) the name of the man John (*talk*) to.
4. I (*think*) you (*make*) a mistake.
5. In summer the sun usually (*shine*), but today it (*rain*).
6. This house (*belong*) to a man who (*write*) books.
7. Mr Brown (*live*) in Bishopton, but at present he is (*stay*) in Edinburgh.
8. I (*want*) to know what David (*do*) now.
9. I (*think*) the man who (*drive*) the car is Mr Brown.
10. Tom (*work*) hard all the week, but today he (*stay*) at home to rest.

I. *Put the word* yet *or* still *into these sentences:*

1. Has he finished his work?
2. I think she is in London.
3. We have five minutes before the bus starts.
4. It isn't five o'clock.
5. I don't know who you are talking about.
6. Is it raining?
7. Tom isn't back from his holiday.
8. Has the train arrived?
9. Does he live in London?
10. Do you know whether he has come home?

J. *Put the word* small, little, less *or* few *into these sentences:*

1. Italy has . . . rain during the summer.
2. . . . people learn languages easily.
3. Will you have a . . . more sugar in your tea?
4. Please make . . . noise.
5. The farmer gave the boys a . . . apples.
6. They have a large farm and a . . . one.
7. He has a . . . sum of money in the bank.
8. She is a very nice . . . girl.
9. He has . . . money than he had last year.
10. The Stansburys live a . . . miles from Bishopton.

K. (a) *Wherever possible make the nouns and pronouns in these sentences feminine:*

1. He met his brother in the street.
2. This is his son.
3. Mr Brown's brother lives in Manchester.
4. I know Mr Jones: his son and my brother are friends.
5. The boy went to the theatre with his father.

(b) *Wherever possible make the nouns and pronouns in these sentences masculine:*

1. She had lost her pen, so she borrowed her sister's.
2. The woman said she was tired, so my wife looked after her.
3. The children went with their mother for a walk in the town.
4. The actress played her part very cleverly.
5. She called the waitress and asked her for more wine.

L. *Put the correct form* it is, it was, there is, there are, there was, etc. *into these sentences:*

1. ... very warm in Bishopton yesterday.
2. ... any sugar in my tea?
3. ... one hundred pence in a pound.
4. ... time for us to go home.
5. ... six rooms in this house.
6. ... easy to lose your way in London.
7. ... a bright fire in the room when we arrived.
8. ... Sunday tomorrow.
9. ... time for you to get to the station if you start now.
10. Years ago ... easier to pass this examination than ... today.

M. *Put the word* want, like, wish, *or* need *into these sentences:*

1. I'm hungry and I ... my dinner.
2. I ... we lived in London instead of in the country.
3. She doesn't ... too much sugar in her tea.
4. Do you ... our new house?
5. His bicycle ... some new tyres.
6. I ... I had more money.
7. What do you ...? I ... a packet of cigarettes, please.
8. Which do you ... better, summer or winter?
9. Do you ... to see the manager, sir?
10. Would you ... to have dinner with us?

N. *In the following sentences the noun in italics is used without an article* a *or the. Write sentences of your own using these nouns, first with* a *and then with* the.

   1. *Books* are sold in this shop.
   2. *Man* has lived in this world for thousands of years.
   3. *Eggs* are cheap during the summer.
   4. *Dogs* are not allowed in this garden.
   5. He was always careful because he was afraid of *fire.*
   6. Some children enjoy *school,* some do not.
   7. *Children* should be seen and not heard.
   8. *Farms* are busy places in summer.
   9. Many people eat *fish* on Fridays.
  10. *Glass* is easily broken.

O. *Write ten sentences, each using a word for a kind of food or drink.*

P. *Write a letter from David Brown to his friend Geoffrey Dixon at New College, Oxford, in which David tells his friend about the Brown family's day at the races.*

Q. *Put the word* since *or* for *into these sentences:*

   1. He has been in Scotland . . . last October.
   2. I have lived in London . . . three years.
   3. We stayed with the Browns . . . two weeks.
   4. Have you seen her . . . last week?
   5. I haven't read this book . . . I was a boy.
   6. He hasn't read a book . . . years.
   7. She will live in Edinburgh . . . three months.
   8. Mr Brown has travelled to London every morning . . . 1960.
   9. How much English have you learnt . . . you came to England?
  10. She sat there without speaking . . . two hours.

Another Meaning of Engaged

"He's a very good talker," said the man in the shop when he sold the parrot to my friend John. But when John got the parrot home, it wouldn't say a word. So he decided to teach it.

He began with "Hello". If the bird couldn't learn that, it would never learn anything.

"Hello, hello, hello!" said John, standing in front of the parrot and speaking very clearly. The parrot put its head under its wing and said nothing.

"Hello, hello, hello!" The parrot still said nothing.

"Hello, hello, HELLO!" shouted John, becoming more and more angry.

At last the parrot looked up. "Number engaged," it said crossly, and put its head back under its wing.

parrot ('parət)   wing (wiŋ)

LESSON 13

David Visits the Houses of Parliament

DURING the Easter holidays David visited the Houses of Parliament at Westminster. David's father and Philip Turner, the Member of Parliament for Bishopton, are old friends, and one day Mr Turner asked David if he would like to look round the Houses of Parliament. Of course, David was very pleased, and the visit was arranged for the following Monday. The M.P. explained that the visit must be on Monday because he had put in for a ticket for the

Strangers' Gallery on that day, so that David could listen to a debate in the House of Commons.

David arrived at Westminster at half past eleven and went to the entrance in the Victoria Tower, near Westminster Hall. The policeman at the door would not let him in, but when he said he was meeting Mr Philip Turner, the M.P. for Bishopton, he was asked to wait in a little room near the door. Soon Mr Turner arrived and their tour began.

He was taken first through long galleries with painted walls to the House of Lords, splendid with red leather and gold. He saw the Throne on which the Queen sits when she opens Parliament, and the Woolsack (it really is a sack of wool) on which the Lord Chancellor sits. He also saw the library of the House of Lords, with its rows and rows of old books and comfortable red leather arm-chairs.

Next he was taken to the House of Commons. Its green leather seats were not so fine as the red and gold of the House of Lords, but David found it more interesting. Here was the Speaker's Chair with the switch that puts on the light in the clock tower above 'Big Ben', to tell Londoners that Parliament is meeting. From here they moved to the wide, empty Westminster Hall, built by William II in 1092. Here the Law Courts met for many centuries, and it is sometimes used today for great state events.

It was now lunch-time and Mr Turner took David along with him for lunch in the famous restaurant which looks out on to the Terrace and the River Thames. In summer Members often invite their friends to have tea on the Terrace.

David enjoyed his lunch, and while they were eating, Mr Turner pointed out famous people who were sitting at other tables. David thought he would like to be an M.P. one day, and work in what has been called 'the finest club in the world'.

After lunch Mr Turner told David that the House would soon be sitting, so he must say good-bye. But first he took David to the Strangers' Gallery. David gave up his ticket and was taken to a seat in the gallery from which he could look down on what was happening in the House of Commons below.

Facing him was the Speaker. Above the Speaker there is a clock on the wall; behind is the seat which is kept for the heir to the throne. No King or Queen of England is allowed to enter the House of Commons. In front of the Speaker, clerks sat at green-covered tables, and on the seats on either side sat the Members, the Government on the Speaker's right, the Opposition on his left. David was amused to see Members on the front seats sitting with their feet on the table in front of them. Some members seemed asleep; others were talking to those sitting next to them. Members were coming in and out all the time, everyone bowing to the Speaker as he came in or out.

If the Members liked what a speaker was saying they shouted "Hear, hear!"; if they did not like it they shouted "No!" Once the Members on the other side became angry and shouted "Shame!" and "Sit down!" until the Speaker told them to stop. When there was a question to be decided, all the Members voted. To do this they went out through two doors at the side. Those who thought 'yes' went through one door; those who thought 'no' through the other. As they went through the doors they were counted. Then they all came back and the Speaker was told how many there were on each side; and so the matter was decided.

David listened to the debate until late in the afternoon. It was all very interesting, but not quite what he had expected. As he went home by train to Bishopton he thought that he had learnt a lot about the English way of life. It had been a day to remember.

CONVERSATION

(At the entrance to the Houses of Parliament)

MR TURNER: Hello, David. Nice to see you. They told me you were waiting for me.

DAVID: It's very good of you to find time for me, sir. I don't want to put you to a lot of trouble. I expect you're very busy.

MR TURNER: Yes, there's plenty to do when you're a Member of Parliament. One has to be careful not to take on more than one can manage. Is this your first visit to the House?

DAVID: Yes.

MR TURNER: Well, let's start with the House of Lords. I don't come here often, of course, but I have seen the Queen opening Parliament, and what a wonderful sight it is! I expect you have seen it on television. All the members of the House of Lords are here in their brightly-coloured robes. As the Queen comes in and takes her place on the Throne, all the lights are suddenly turned up brightly. It is really beautiful—something you can never forget.

DAVID: Why does the Lord Chancellor sit on a Woolsack?

MR TURNER: Because years ago wool was the most important thing we produced in this country. I suppose today he should sit on a sack of coal or a piece of machinery, although that wouldn't be very comfortable. We go through this door to the House of Commons.

DAVID: It doesn't look so splendid as the House of Lords, but really it is much more important, isn't it?

MR TURNER: Oh, yes. The real government of the country is carried on from here. That's the Speaker's Chair, and that's where the Prime Minister sits.

DAVID: And where do you sit, sir?

MR TURNER: Well, I'm not a very important Member, so I sit anywhere I can. I usually like to sit on one of those seats up there. Now let's have a look at some of the places people don't usually see when they are taken round by the ordinary guides.

· · · ·

MR TURNER: What do you think of this?

DAVID: What a delightful room. I like the leather arm-chairs by the fire.

MR TURNER: This is the House of Lords Library. It has a wonderful collection of books. And this is the restaurant. We'll come back here later.

DAVID: Where is the place where the House of Commons used to meet?

MR TURNER: That's St Stephen's Hall. For centuries the House met here, until the fire in 1834.

DAVID: It seems very small and narrow, doesn't it?

MR TURNER: Yes. But there weren't so many Members in those days. This is Westminster Hall. It was built in 1092.

DAVID: What a huge place.

MR TURNER: Look at the roof. That wooden roof is seven hundred years old. This hall is still used sometimes for great state events. And now I expect you're hungry and ready for lunch. The cooking is better on some days than on others! When we can't put up with it, we grumble to the Kitchen Committee and they try to do something about it.

· · · ·

DAVID: Thank you very much for making my visit so interesting—and for my excellent lunch. I hope I haven't taken up too much of your time.

MR TURNER: It's sometimes nice to put pleasure before work. What are you going to do when you leave university? Are you going to take after your father and go into the bank?

DAVID: No, I don't think so. It depends on how well I do in my degree examination. As a matter of fact, I should like to take up politics when I have finished my three years at Oxford.

MR TURNER: And become a Member of Parliament, eh? Well, it's an interesting profession. I may have the pleasure of seeing you here one day. But mind you come in on the right side! Now you must excuse me. I have to put in some time writing letters before the House meets. Here is your ticket for the Strangers' Gallery. The policeman will tell you where to go. I hope you enjoy the debate. Give my good wishes to your father.

DAVID: Yes I will, sir. Thank you again; and good-bye.

SENTENCE PATTERNS

49. Case in Pronouns

Case is a change in the noun or pronoun to show the work it is doing in the sentence.

There are three cases in English:

The case of the subject to a verb.

The case of the direct or indirect object to a verb or after a preposition.

The case of possession.

In nouns, the only case-change is in the possessive (see Sentence Pattern 35, page 124, The Possessive of Nouns).

In pronouns the case-changes are these:

Subject	Object or after Preposition	Possessive
I	me	my, mine
you	you	your, yours
he, she, it	him, her, it	his, her, hers, its
we	us	our, ours
you	you	your, yours
they	them	their, theirs
who	whom	whose, whose

Notice that *you* has the same form as subject and object, singular and plural; *it* has the same form as subject and object. In the possessive, the first form is really an adjective, the second is a pronoun.

Subject to a verb

I live in a small house.
You have a book in your hand.
He has caught the train.
She likes reading.
When the carpet has been taken up, *it* is then cleaned.
We have not been up to London for three months.
You may all go home now.
They jumped into the water, one after another.
People *who* live in glass houses should not throw stones.

Object to a verb

Mr Robinson took *me* to the theatre.
Did Mrs Brown see *you* in town?
Susan met *him* at a party.
Tom likes *her* very much.
Mr Brown bought a new car and drove *it* home.
Mr Brook left *us* at the station.
Did Mr Carter invite *you* all to dinner?
The children were lost, so Mr Brown took *them* home.
Susan doesn't like the man *whom* she met last night.

After a preposition

The policeman spoke to *me*.
Did he buy a book from *you*.
The dog was running after *him*.
Mr Brown went with *her* to the theatre.
When the dog barked the children ran away from *it*.
The other children threw sand at *us*.
The boy beside *you* is Susan's brother.
The teacher sat down among *them* and started to talk.
We have just seen the man from *whom* we bought this house.

Possessive

This is *my* house.   This house is *mine*.
That is *your* book.   That book is *yours*.
He showed me *his* garden.   That garden is *his*.
She has lost *her* gloves.   Are those gloves *hers*?
The dog has lost *its* collar.   Is this *its*? (More often: Is this *his*?)
We are proud of *our* car.   This car is *ours*.
Have you booked *your* seats?   Are these seats *yours*?
They met *their* friends at the station.   Are all these clothes
    theirs?
This is the girl *whose* parents live next door.
We have found someone's book but we don't know *whose*.

Notice that in these pairs of sentences, the first possessive is an
adjective, the second is a pronoun.

50.   Collective Nouns

A collective noun is one used for a collection of people or things.

There was a noisy *crowd* in the street.
We went to listen to this famous *orchestra*.
The whole of David's *school* has gone on holiday.
It was a good match, and the best *team* has won.
The teacher told the *class* it was time to go home.
There is a whole *library* of books here to choose from.

Parliament meets every afternoon at two o'clock.
There were two or three hundred trees in the *wood*.

Other collective nouns are:

company, family, government, college, university, firm, club, committee.

51.   Phrasal Verbs—*Put, Take*

Idiom plays a large part in English today, particularly in spoken English. A few simple words are used to give a large number of different meanings by adding prepositions or adverbs. Often the prepositions and adverbs added in this way seem to have quite lost the meaning they once had. This idiomatic use of 'Phrasal Verbs' is not easy, but these verbs are used so often in English today that sooner or later they must be learnt—and the sooner the better!

We begin with *Put* and *Take*.

Put

Put away

You may put your books away now and go home.
   (*or* You may put away your books . . .)
She put the letters away in a cupboard for safety.
He put his bicycle away in the garage and came in to tea.
He has been putting money away in the bank for years.

Put aside

David is putting aside some money each week for when he goes to Oxford.
Put this aside until you need it.
I put the letter aside somewhere, and now I can't find it.

Put back

Put this book back where it came from.
You should always put things back where you found them.
Your watch is fast. Put it back five minutes.
He put the glass back on the table after he had drunk the wine.

Put before

It is sometimes nice to put pleasure before work.

I'll put all the ideas before you and then you can make up your mind.

A man who wants to be a manager before he has learnt the job is putting the cart before the horse.

Put in

He has put in for a new car, but he will have to wait for it.

Tom puts in a lot of hard work at the factory.

Mr Nokes has put in a new fireplace for Mrs Brown.

If you put five pence in this machine, you will get some chocolate.

Put on

Put on your coat. It's going to rain.

If you have early morning tea at a hotel they will put it on the bill.

In England we used to put the clocks on one hour in the spring, and back one hour in the autumn.

Put off

Never put off till tomorrow what you can do today.

When I found a hair in my soup it quite put me off.

When he came to visit us we put him off by saying we were just going out.

Put out

The rude boy put out his tongue at his parents.

She nearly fell, but I put out my hand to help her.

Always put out the lights before you go to bed.

The man was singing loudly in the hotel, so they put him out.

Put to

He put the question to each M.P. in turn.

He put me to so much trouble that I became angry.

If they had put it to me clearly, I would have agreed to what they asked.

Put up

We put up our umbrellas when it began to rain.
Can you put me up for the night?
Seaside hotels usually put their prices up in the summer.
They put up the notice, so that we could all read it.

Put up with

I won't put up with his rudeness any longer.
I have put up with this noise for long enough.

Take

Take away

The waiter took away the empty plates.
Please take this dog away.
If you take away five from eight you have three.

Take after

Does he take after his father or his mother?
Neither of his parents is tall; I don't know who he takes after.

Take in

She will take in any animal she finds without a home.
We thought the watch was gold, but I'm afraid we were taken in.
He talks so quickly that I can't take in all he says.

Take on

They have taken on more than a hundred new workmen this
    week.
I think she has taken on more than she can manage.

Take off

A man takes off his hat when he meets a lady.
Take the kettle off the gas as soon as it boils.
She arrived a minute or two before the aeroplane took off.

Take out

I will take you out for a run in the car this afternoon.

He took out a handkerchief and wiped his face.

You are not allowed to take out more than two books at a time from the library.

Take up

He has taken up cricket since he came to Bishopton.

For a small house you should buy furniture that will not take up too much room.

NEW WORDS

captain (ˈkaptin)

collar (ˈkolə)

collection (kəˈlekʃn)

committee (kəˈmiti)

court (koɪt)

debate (diˈbeit)

degree (diˈgriɪ)

Easter (ˈiːstə)

gallery (ˈgaləri)

heir (eə)

law (loɪ)

leaf, leaves (liːf, liːvz)

machinery (məˈʃiːnəri)

member (ˈmembə)

notice (ˈnoutis)

opposition (opəˈziʃn)

politics (ˈpolitiks)

profession (prəˈfeʃn)

robes (roubz)

row (rou)

sack (sak)

shame (ʃeim)

sight (sait)

state (steit)

stranger (ˈstreindʒə)

switch (switʃ)

terrace (ˈteris)

throne (θroun)

tour (tuə)

bow, bowed (bau, baud)

count, counted (kaunt, ˈkauntid)

depend, depended (diˈpend, diˈpendid)

enter, entered (ˈentə, ˈentəd)

produce, produced (prəˈdjuːs, prəˈdjuːst)

vote, voted (vout, ˈvoutid)

amused (əˈmjuːzd)

aside (əˈsaid)

below (biˈlou)

delightful (diˈlaitful)

facing (ˈfeisiŋ)

opposite (ˈopəzit)

ordinary (ˈoɪdinri)

wooden (ˈwudn)

Idioms

(For idioms with phrasal verbs see Sentence Patterns)
   Hear, hear! ('hiə 'hiə)
   try to do something about it ('trai tə du 'sʌmθiŋ ə'baut it)
   Give my good wishes to . . . ('giv mai gud 'wiʃiz tə)
   it depends . . . (it di'pendz)

EXERCISES

A. *Answer these questions in sentences:*

   1. What are the names of the two Houses of Parliament?
   2. Where do visitors sit to watch debates in Parliament?
   3. On what does the Lord Chancellor sit in the House of Lords, and why?
   4. Where does the Queen sit when she opens Parliament?
   5. What does the Speaker do?
   6. How can Londoners tell when a meeting of the House is on?
   7. Who built Westminster Hall, and when?
   8. Which English person is not allowed to enter the House of Commons? Why do you think this is so?
   9. How do Members of Parliament vote?
   10. What does David want to do when he leaves the university?

B. *Use these phrasal verbs in sentences different from those given in the Sentence Patterns:*

   put back; put on; put off; put out; put up; take away; take in; take on; take off; take out.

C. *Use the correct form of the pronoun in these sentences. The subject form is given in brackets.*

   1. David is ill and the doctor has come to see (*he*).
   2. We were talking to the people at (*who*) house we stayed last week.

3. He is well known to my father and (*I*).
4. Is this the man (*who*) was in your house yesterday?
5. This book is (*you*), and that book is (*I*).
6. (*She*) says this is (*she*) book, and (*she*) thinks all those are (*she*), too.
7. (*You*) can leave this work to Tom and (*I*).
8. (*We*) gave (*they*) (*we*), and (*they*) gave (*we*) (*they*).
9. (*She*) garden is much prettier than (*we*).
10. Show (*I*) the man from (*who*) (*you*) bought (*you*) new car.

D. *Write about a visit to a famous building or other place of interest that you know well.*

E. *Add question-tags to these sentences:*
   1. I am a silly girl.
   2. You won't be late.
   3. She found her book.
   4. Tom hasn't finished his work yet.
   5. He can go home now.
   6. Children usually like sweets.
   7. You daren't jump off that wall.
   8. He didn't do his homework last night.
   9. They got home before it started to rain.
   10. We're not going to bed yet.

F. *Make these sentences singular:*
   1. Our wives work hard and so do we.
   2. The men work in the fields while the women look after the houses.
   3. Our friends' children often come to stay with us.
   4. In these towns the boys' schools are better than the girls' schools.
   5. They had three weeks' holiday during the summer.
   6. The leaves have fallen from the trees.
   7. They have invited their sons' friends to tea.
   8. We caught some fish in the streams.

9. They like some sandwiches with their tea, but they don't want any cakes.
10. If we were doing this work, we should be more careful.

G. *Fill in the missing preposition/adverbs:*

1. They travelled . . . train . . . London . . . Manchester.
2. He took . . . his pen to write . . . his brother.
3. She walked . . . the room . . . her friend, who was standing . . . the fire.
4. I found the letter . . . some books . . . the table . . . the sitting-room.
5. The dog jumped . . . the wall . . . a stream on the other side, but he soon got . . . . . . the water.
6. He climbed . . . the window and walked . . . the carpet . . . his dirty boots.
7. I haven't seen him . . . this morning, but I expect him home . . . midnight.
8. Most seaside hotels put . . . their prices . . . the summer months.
9. He took . . . his shoes and threw them . . . a corner . . . the room.
10. Can you find . . . if our friends have arrived . . . London? They set . . . from Edinburgh early this morning . . . train.
11. Did she go . . . the theatre . . . herself, or did she go . . . some friends?
12. When the taxi came quickly . . . the corner, it ran . . . another car and a wheel came . . .

H. *Put these sentences into reported speech after a phrase with a verb of saying or telling or asking. E.g. He said that . . . He told them to . . . :*

1. Close the window!
2. We have been here for two hours.
3. When did you arrive in London?
4. Where are you going for your holiday this summer?

5. Stop talking, and start work.
6. Yesterday I told Miss Jones what to do, and she has forgotten again.
7. Where do you stay when you are in London?
8. It's my birthday tomorrow, so I'm having a holiday.
9. Finish your work and hand in your books.
10. Have you seen any good plays since you arrived in England?

I. *Give the meaning of the verb* have *in each of these sentences, and then turn each into a question:*

1. David has a holiday every Saturday.
2. Tom has a new car.
3. Susan has to start work at nine o'clock.
4. You have some matches in your pocket.
5. They have snow in Switzerland every year.
6. We have to go home now.
7. He always has milk in his coffee.
8. They have some good pictures in their house.
9. We shall have to hurry.
10. He has gone home.

J. *Give the correct form of the verb in brackets:*

1. Have you ever (*be*) to Spain?
2. They (*go*) to France last summer.
3. David (*be*) nineteen on his next birthday.
4. Mr Brown (*finish*) his work and is on his way home.
5. David was pleased when he (*choose*) captain of his cricket team.
6. I (*go*) to London next week if the weather (*be*) fine.
7. I (*remember*) the first time I (*see*) him.
8. David (*walk*) down Whitehall yesterday when he (*meet*) a friend.
9. I (*write*) to him several times, but he never (*write*) to me.
10. How long have you (*live*) in London?

K. *Supply short answers to the following questions:*

1. Do you walk to the station every morning?
2. Has David finished his homework yet?
3. Are you a good swimmer?
4. Are you the best swimmer in the world?
5. Dare he jump off this high wall?
6. Did Tom pass his examination?
7. Can you speak Spanish?
8. Will you be in London next week?
9. Is Cardiff in Scotland?
10. May I close the window, please?

L. *Finish these sentences with conditional clauses beginning with if or unless:*

1. I shall spend my holiday in Ireland this year . . .
2. I walk to the station every morning . . .
3. I should be more careful . . .
4. You can't drive a car in England . . .
5. The roads are very crowded at week-ends . . .
6. You would learn more quickly . . .
7. People enjoy going to the theatre . . .
8. They would shop in Oxford Street more often . . .
9. You won't catch that bus . . .
10. I should be very angry . . .

M. *Make imperative sentences telling someone to do the following:*

1. To pick up a book.
2. To take off his coat.
3. To pass you the sugar.
4. Not to make a noise.
5. Not to talk during the lesson.
6. Not to leave the door open.
7. To open the window.
8. To switch off the light.
9. Not to throw matches on the floor.
10. Not to spend all his money at once.

N. *Put these sentences into the passive:*

1. Someone has eaten all the apples.
2. People say this tree is a thousand years old.
3. No one has cut this grass since last week.
4. They asked him to speak about Wales and the Welsh people.
5. Somebody built this castle many centuries ago.
6. You mustn't tear pages out of the answer books.
7. They have chosen you to play for the school.
8. It is time they closed this shop for the night.
9. No one has ever climbed this mountain before.
10. Someone married her when she was only eighteen.

O. *Put the verbs in these sentences into the correct past tense:*

1. This shop now (*close*) for the night.
2. He (*walk*) across the road when he (*run over*) by a car.
3. I (*finish*) my work before our friends (*arrive*).
4. We (*arrive*) at the station after the train (*leave*).
5. He (*will*) not do what I (*ask*).
6. If I (*have*) more money I (*buy*) you a nicer present.
7. Mr Turner (*talk*) to David while they (*have*) lunch.
8. He (*write*) several books about the English language.
9. He (*live*) in London all his life, but now he (*go*).
10. He (*promised*) a new bicycle on his next birthday.

P. *Give the full date for the day before and the day after each of the following:*

1. Sunday 5th May 1961.
2. Friday 28th February 1964.
3. Monday 30th June 1963.
4. Wednesday 1st October 1966.
5. Saturday 1st January 1960.

Q. *Add a clause to complete each of these sentences:*

1. . . . because it is already very late.
2. . . . as you have no money.

P.D.E. II—7*

3. . . . because he is too young.
4. . . . because we have a holiday today.
5. As you are a stranger in this town . . .
6. . . . because she is a good cook.
7. As he has worked so hard this term . . .
8. . . . because they didn't want to catch cold.
9. Because the weather is so fine today . . .
10. . . . because there was no food in the house.

R.   *Write a composition telling what happened to David and some
of the things he saw when he visited the Houses of Parliament.
Read the passage on page 184 again before you start, but do
not take sentences from it while you are writing.*

Tongue Twisters

Repeat these quickly several times:

She sells sea-shells on the sea-shore.

How much wood would a wood-pecker peck, if a wood-
pecker would peck wood?

Round and round the rugged rock,
The ragged rascal ran.

LESSON 14

The White Cliffs of Dover

MARGRIT and Edouard Erling are on their way to visit their friends, the Browns. They have been to England several times before. They usually come by air, but this time they decided they would try coming by sea.

"I daresay we shall be sea-sick, but I'll try anything once," Margrit had said, when they bought their tickets. And now they were half-way across the Channel, with the sun shining overhead, and the sea as calm and smooth as a lake.

They had set off from their home in Lucerne late the evening before and travelled across France all through the night, arriving at Calais in time to go on board the cross-Channel boat waiting at the quay. Having seen their suitcases put away in one of the luggage-racks, they went straight down to the restaurant for breakfast—an English breakfast: bacon and eggs, toast and marmalade and tea or coffee.

Coming up on deck after breakfast, they saw that the coast of France was disappearing behind them (a sailor would say 'astern') and in front ('ahead'), shining white in the bright sunlight, were the cliffs of England—the white cliffs of Dover. Margrit and Edouard joined the many passengers who were leaning on the rails watching the English coast coming nearer and nearer. Some of them were seeing England for the first time; some were coming home after living abroad perhaps for years; most were holiday-makers visiting England or coming back after a holiday in France, or Spain, or Italy.

At last the cliffs closed round them, and they were in Dover Harbour. Giving up their landing cards they stepped on to the quay. It seemed much more exciting than just getting out of a plane at London Airport. At the entrance to the customs office their passports were checked. Inside they found their porter waiting for them with their bags on the long wooden tables behind which stood the customs officers. Margrit thought how smart they were. But when she looked at the cold blue eyes and unsmiling face of the customs officer she read the card he handed her, and answered his questions carefully and truthfully. She told him about the bottle of scent and other small presents she had brought for Mrs Brown and Susan, and Edouard told him about the bottle of brandy and the box of cigars he had for Mr Brown. The officer did not ask them to open their cases and in another minute they were through the gate, on the platform, and sitting in their reserved seats on the London train.

Travelling through the Kent countryside, they watched

the fields and hedges roll by the carriage windows, looking fresh and green in the sunshine. As they got nearer to London, fields gave way to small country houses, then streets of brick houses, and last of all the tall towers of Battersea Power Station and so across the Thames and into Victoria Station.

As the boat-train pulled in, Margrit and Edouard saw David Brown waiting for them on the platform. Edouard suggested they should have a meal in the West End before going on to Bishopton. David was just going to call a taxi when Margrit said she would rather go by 'tube'. She thought travelling by Underground was part of the fun of coming to London. So, leaving their bags in the Left Luggage Office, they went on the District Line to Charing Cross. This line runs mostly on the surface, and goes underground only in the centre of London. At Charing Cross they changed to the Bakerloo Line. They followed coloured lights along tunnels till they came to the train for Piccadilly. After an excellent lunch in a restaurant, they travelled back to Victoria by bus, and caught a local train to Bishopton.

Mrs Brown was waiting for them at the station with the car, and when they got home, they were ready for anything the holiday might bring.

CONVERSATION

(On board the cross-Channel boat. Margrit and Edouard Erling come up on deck from the restaurant)

EDOUARD: We are more than half-way across so now we must try to talk nothing but English. No more French until we're on our way home.

MARGRIT: All right. I think we can manage without dictionaries this time. It's good practice, isn't it?

EDOUARD: I feel better for my breakfast. There's a lot to be said for the English breakfast, especially when you've been travelling all night.

MARGRIT: Yes. What a lovely day! What are all those people looking at, over there?

EDOUARD: The English coast I expect. Let's go and look.

MARGRIT: Beautiful, isn't it? We needn't have worried about being sea-sick. The sea's as calm as a lake. Is that Dover, over there?

EDOUARD: Yes. That'll be the lighthouse at the mouth of the harbour. We'll soon be in now.

MARGRIT: How far is it across?

EDOUARD: About twenty miles.

MARGRIT: What a difference that twenty miles makes. We've come hundreds of miles from home, but this last little piece of water seems to separate two different worlds.

EDOUARD: I expect that's why the English have always loved the sea. Their little island and all that it means to them needs the sea to keep it what it is. And even the coming of the aeroplane doesn't seem to make any difference to their ideas. They still believe that nothing can really hurt them so long as their ships are masters of the Channel.

MARGRIT: But you can't help liking them—most of them, anyway. They make you angry sometimes when they think that one Englishman is as good as three people from any other country; but they're wonderfully kind at heart—especially to foreigners.

EDOUARD: Do you remember the man who walked three miles out of his way with us when we got lost?

MARGRIT: Yes, and the woman up in the Lake District who gave us a meal and beds for the night when we had missed our last train, and wouldn't take any money. You always feel so safe in England too.

EDOUARD: I wonder why that is. I think it's because you really *are* safe. Even criminals seldom carry guns and the police never do. It's three hundred years since there's been any serious fighting in England. And most English people believe in minding their own business and letting other people mind theirs. 'Live and let live' they call it.

MARGRIT: And they're such *orderly* people, too. Look at the way they line up for a bus, or wait quietly in turn to go into a cinema or dance-hall. And look how carefully most of them drive.

EDOUARD: I think their careful driving is partly due to their roads. They'd all be killed if they drove as fast as we do along some of their narrow, twisting country roads.

MARGRIT: There may be a lot of things wrong with England, but I love coming here, all the same. I love the bright colour of the buses in the London streets and the bus-conductors calling, "Any more fares, please?" I love all the little houses on the edge of the towns with men working in their gardens at the week-end. I love the square church towers, and the tidy green hedges, and the cows in the fields.

EDOUARD: You're quite a poet. Don't forget the rain and the open fires which burn your knees while your back freezes in the cold weather.

MARGRIT: Yes, it's a pity, but you can't have everything. And lots of new houses in England have central heating now. Anyway, I like open fires. The trouble is, the English can't get servants to look after their houses. English girls won't go as maids, and if it wasn't for the Swiss, German, French, Spanish and Italian girls who come over to do housework in order to learn English, I don't know what they'd do.

EDOUARD: We're almost in now, so we'd better get near the side so that we can find a porter as soon as they come on board. The tide's high, so we'll be going on shore from the lower deck. Come on. Let's line up like the English!

SENTENCE PATTERNS

52.   Phrasal Verbs—*Come, Go*

Come

Come across

When my friend saw me he came across to speak to me.
We came across a little shop where you can buy books and
   pictures.

Come down

I'll come down as soon as I'm dressed.
They've come down from London for the week-end.
The cost of petrol has come down since I was last in England.

Come for

The taxi came for us at 8 o'clock.
The milkman is at the door. He's come for his money.

Come in

What time did you come in last night?
Open the door. The dog wants to come in.
You can't come in; the carriage is full.

Come on

David is coming on well with his school work.
We looked for somewhere to stay, as night was coming on.
Come on! Hurry up!

Come off

When David ran into a wall, a wheel of his bicycle came off.
They are planning a holiday in Italy, but I don't think it'll come
   off (happen).

Come out

When does your new book come out?
Boys and girls, come out to play!
He's been in hospital, but he comes out tomorrow.

Come round

The Browns are coming round for a game of cards this evening.
He didn't agree with me at first, but he's coming round to my
    way of thinking.

Come up

Mrs Brown and Susan are coming up to London on Saturday.
When the doctor arrives, tell him to come up.

Go

Go away

They are not at home. They have gone away for a holiday.
Go away! I'm busy.
They don't live here now. They've gone away.

Go back

I've lost my gloves. I must go back and look for them.
If she's a rude child, she'll have to go back home.

Go down

We're going down to Brighton for a few days.
It's very cold today, and the temperature's still going down.

Go for

I think you'd better go for the doctor.
They are going for a walk in the country.
How long are you going for?
I didn't expect the dog to go for you like that.

Go in

You can't take all that luggage. It won't go in the car.
I hear he's going in for farming.

Go off

The party went off very well.
She has gone off to see her friends in Italy.
He went off to sleep as soon as he got into bed.
He was surprised when the gun went off.

Go on

Susan and Tom were going on to a party after the theatre.
As we were in a hurry, we did not stop for a meal, but went on.
The party went on so long, that they missed their last train home.

Go out

Children are sometimes frightened when the lights go out and they are in the dark.
I don't think I shall go out today.
The fire has gone out, and the room is cold.
Where's Tom? He's gone out.

Go through

I was very ill. I shouldn't like to go through that again.
He went through all the letters in his pocket before he found the one he wanted.
She went through all her money in a year.

Go up

Mr Brown goes up to London every day.
The price of coal has gone up again.
It's bed-time. You children must go up.

Go with

Do you think this new hat goes with my coat?
Red wine goes with meat, and white wine with chicken.

Go without

As you have come home late, you must go without your dinner.
I'm afraid we shall have to go without an expensive holiday this
  year.

53.   Participle Phrases

Notice that the subject of the main clause must be the same as the
subject of the participle phrase.

Coming up on deck, they saw that the sun was shining.
Turning the corner, they met an old friend of theirs.
Hearing a noise, he went to the door to see who it was.
Seeing an open space, he left his car there.
Finding the room empty, Mrs Brown sat down by the fire to read.
Working hard all the morning, Mr Brown finished his gardening
  by lunch time.
Not knowing the way, they decided to ask a policeman.
Living next door to them, we came to know them well.
Looking through his pockets, she found the missing letter.
Leaning over the ship's rail, they could see the white cliffs of
  Dover.
Leaving their bags with a porter, they went ashore.

54.   Exclamations

What . . .!

What a lovely day!
What a long time you've been!
What a nice girl she is!
What a beautiful garden you have!
What a silly boy you are!
What a lot of people come to this restaurant!
What a pity you have to go now!
What a good thing he wasn't driving the new car!
What a fuss she made about the torn dress!
What rude children they are!

How . . .!

How nice of you to come!
How silly of me to forget!
How kind you are to me!
How they enjoyed themselves at the seaside!
How easy it is to make a mistake!
How tall you have grown since I saw you last!
How strange that we should both arrive on the same day!
How beautiful the country-side looks in early summer!
How hard you have worked all day!
How the crowd shouted when the last goal was scored!

55.   Indefinite Pronouns—*Some, Any*, etc.

(a) *Some* is used in affirmative statements and *any* is used in negative statements and questions.

> I have *some* eggs in my basket.
> I haven't *any* eggs in my basket.
> Have you *any* eggs in your basket?

(b) *Some*—We do not know who, or what, or how many—all we are told is that it or they exist.

> *Any*—Again we are not told who, or what, or how many the speaker or writer is referring to, but this time we do not even know whether it or they exist at all.

> May I have *some* apples? (I'm sure you have apples in your shop)
> Have you *any* apples? (I don't know if you have apples in your shop)

(c) *Anyone, anybody, anything, anywhere*
There is no limit to the persons, things or places.

> *Anyone* can do this.
> Has *anybody* seen my brother?

You can do *anything* if you try hard enough.
You will never find the ring. It might be *anywhere*.

Someone, somebody, something, somewhere
It is certain that there is a person, thing, or place, but we do not know who or what or where it is.

Someone has taken my car.
There is *somebody* waiting for you outside.
Something must be done at once.
I shall go on looking. The ring must be *somewhere*.

(*d*) Indefinite Pronouns followed by the Infinitive
   *Something, anything, nothing, someone (somebody), anyone
      (anybody), no one (nobody)*

She has something to tell you.
Have you anything to do?
She has nothing to wear.
I am looking for somebody to help me.
We have sent somebody to fetch him.
Have you anyone to look after you?
There wasn't anybody to be seen.
We saw no one to speak to.
There was nobody to listen to him.

(*e*) Indefinite Pronouns followed by *else*

I have something else to show you.
Is there anything else in the cupboard?
There was nothing else in her bag.
She knew there was somebody else in the room.
I am sure someone else lives in the house with him.
Has anyone else been here today?
She wouldn't speak to anybody else.
No one else would believe his story.
I have invited nobody else but you.

NEW WORDS

airport ('eəpoːt)
board (boːd)
brandy ('brandi)
brick (brik)
central heating ('sentrl 'hiːtiŋ)
centre ('sentə)
cigar (si'gaː)
cliff (klif)
coast (koust)
countryside ('kʌntrisaid)
criminal ('kriminl)
customs ('kʌstəmz)
deck (dek)
dictionary ('dikʃənri)
gun (gʌn)
harbour ('haːbə)
heart (haːt)
island ('ailənd)
knee (niː)
lighter ('laitə)
lighthouse ('laithaus)
luggage-rack ('lʌgidʒrak)
passenger ('pasindʒə)
passport ('paːspoːt)
petrol ('petrl)
plane (plein)
poet ('pouit)
practice ('praktis)
quay (kiː)
sailor ('seilə)
scent (sent)
space (speis)
suit-case ('sjuːtkeis)
surface ('səːfis)

tide (taid)
toast (toust)

check, checked (tʃek, tʃekt)
disappear, disappeared ('disə'piə, 'disə'piəd)
fight, fought (fait, foːt)
freeze, froze, frozen (friːz, frouz, frouzn)
join, joined (dʒoin, dʒoind)
kill, killed (kil, kild)
land, landed (land, 'landid)
plan, planned (plan, pland)
reserve, reserved (ri'zəːv, ri'zəːvd)
separate, separated ('sepəreit, 'sepəreitid)
step, stepped (step, stept)
suggest, suggested (sə'dʒest, sə'dʒestid)
twist, twisted (twist, 'twistid)
wonder, wondered ('wʌndə, 'wʌndəd)

calm (kaːm)
due (djuː)
foreigner ('for'nə)
half-way ('haːf'wei)
local ('loukl)
orderly ('oːdəli)
overhead ('ouvə'hed)
sea-sick ('siːsik)
smooth (smuːð)
square (skweə)
truthfully ('truːθfuli)

Idioms

on their way (ˈon ðeə ˈwei)
I'll try anything once (ail ˈtrai ˈeniθiŋ ˈwʌns)
all through the night (ˈɔːl ˈθru ðə ˈnait)
ready for anything (ˈredi fər ˈeniθiŋ)
to feel better for (tə ˈfiːl ˈbetə fə)
a lot to be said for . . . (ə ˈlot tə bi ˈsed fə)
to have a look (tə ˈhav ə ˈluk)
kind at heart (ˈkaind ət ˈhaːt)
to go out of your way to . . . (tə ˈgou aut əv jə ˈwei tə)
to mind your own business (tə ˈmaind jər ˈoun ˈbiznis)
live and let live (ˈliv ənd ˈlet ˈliv)
to line up (tə ˈlain ˈʌp)

EXERCISES

A. *Answer the following questions in sentences:*

1. Where do Margrit and Edouard live?
2. What did they have for breakfast on the boat?
3. Why does Margrit like England?
4. What did they think was wrong with England and the English?
5. What is the work of a customs officer?
6. What presents had they brought with them?
7. How did Margrit and Edouard know they were getting near to London?
8. Why did they go from Victoria to Piccadilly by Underground?
9. Who was waiting for them when they got to Bishopton?

B. *Use these phrasal verbs in sentences different from those given in the Sentence Patterns:*

come across; come down; come on; come out; come up; go back; go in; go on; go through; go with.

C. *Put the right indefinite pronoun into each of these sentences:*

　　1. We have . . . friends living in this town.
　　2. There aren't . . . mistakes in this exercise.
　　3. Have you . . . sugar in your tea?
　　4. This isn't very difficult; . . . can do it.
　　5. . . . has taken my book from the desk.
　　6. This dress is badly torn; I can't do . . . with it.
　　7. They gave the hungry dog . . . to eat.
　　8. We heard a shout, but when we reached the door there
　　　　was . . . to be seen.
　　9. I found a key, but there was . . . else in the bag.
　10. We have asked . . . to look after him.

D. *Finish these sentences. Remember that the subject of the clause
　　you add must be the same as the subject of the phrase given:*

　　1. Arriving in London late at night . . .
　　2. Not having been to England before . . .
　　3. Keeping out of sight . . .
　　4. Opening the door slowly . . .
　　5. Returning home earlier than usual . . .
　　6. Jumping up from the table . . .
　　7. Shouting angrily . . .
　　8. Not wishing to make a noise . . .
　　9. Standing on the deck of the cross-Channel steamer . . .
　10. Before getting into the railway carriage . . .

E. *Put pronouns or possessive adjectives into these sentences:*

　　1. He has lost . . . book; one day he'll lose . . .
　　2. I don't know whether the coat is . . . or . . .
　　3. This is . . . book; I bought it . . .
　　4. I taught . . . to drive a car; now . . . can drive by . . .
　　5. Where have you left . . . car? . . . is outside the house.
　　6. I hope you all enjoy . . . at the party.
　　7. He had cut . . . with a knife, so he put a handkerchief
　　　　round . . . hand.

8. One can enjoy . . . in . . . own house.
9. I've shown . . . the way. Don't blame . . . if . . . lose . . .
10. . . . friend Tom and . . . met . . . friends at the station and went with . . . to the cinema.

F. *Finish these sentences with clauses of the kind asked for:*

1. You won't pass your examination . . . (*condition*)
2. Susan was late at the office this morning . . . (*reason*)
3. They enjoyed the walk in the country . . . (*concession*)
4. Mrs Brown went to the post office . . . (*time*)
5. You can stay at our house . . . (*time*)
6. The old lady could see quite well . . . (*concession*)
7. Anyone will show you the way . . . (*condition*)
8. They come to England for their holidays every year . . . (*reason*)
9. You will enjoy the National Gallery . . . (*condition*)
10. They are a very happy family . . . (*concession*)

G. *Put the word* mind *or* matter *into these sentences and say what the word means in the sentence:*

1. Do you . . . if I open the window? No, I don't . . . at all.
2. When I saw his face his name came back to my . . .
3. We haven't seen her for a long time. Is anything the . . . with her?
4. Does it . . . what time you get home?
5. I was left at home to . . . the baby.
6. We can't walk there because it's raining. Never . . ., we'll go by bus.
7. It's not an easy . . . to pass this examination.
8. She wants to see me, but I don't know what she has in . . .
9. Does it . . . if you pass this examination? Yes, it . . . a lot.
10. I've made up my . . . to go to Italy for my holiday next year.

H. *Write five sentences using emphasising* -self *pronouns and five sentences using reflexive* -self *pronouns.*

I. *Write a letter from Margrit Erling to her mother in Switzerland, telling about her journey to England.*

J. *Put* a, an, the, *or* some *into these sentences where necessary:*

    1. Susan went to . . . theatre with . . . friend.
    2. . . . people like . . . sugar in . . . tea.
    3. Do you like . . . egg for . . . breakfast.
    4. She likes . . . swimming and . . . dancing, and she also enjoys . . . game of tennis.
    5. What . . . pity . . . sun isn't shining!
    6. Mr Brown brought . . . potatoes and . . . cabbage from . . . garden.
    7. Please tell me . . . time; I haven't . . . watch.
    8. We have . . . beautiful flowers in our garden and . . . tall oak tree.
    9. I want . . . box of . . . matches, . . . cigarettes and . . . best cigarette lighter you have, please.
    10. We went by . . . car to . . . seaside with . . . friends.

K. *Write sentences (ten sentences in all) using these adjectives first in the comparative and then in the superlative form:*

pretty; wonderful; interesting; lazy; bad.

L. *Put the word* too *or* enough *into these sentences:*

(Note: *too* comes before the adjective, *enough* comes after. *Too* has a negative and *enough* a positive meaning)

    1. It was dark to see one's hand in front of one's face.
    2. The ground is hard for digging.
    3. He speaks English well to find his way about.
    4. I got up late this morning to catch the bus.
    5. He was tall to reach the high shelf.

6. It was cold to go swimming.
7. He was tired to work hard.
8. It is early for you to have a meal before you go.
9. I have not been here long to have many friends.
10. This parcel is heavy to go by post.

The Shortest Way

A passenger boat was moving slowly in a thick fog. On deck an old lady, rather frightened, asked a sailor:

"How far are we from land?"

"Half a mile," he answered.

"Where?" said the old lady.

"Straight down."

fog (fog)

LESSON 15

Cricket at Lord's

THERE is always a big crowd at Lord's for the Test Match against Australia, but on this fine, sunny afternoon the whole of London seemed to be packed into the space around this famous piece of flat green grass. The wicket, which had been cut and rolled and looked after for weeks in preparation for this day, was at its best—a fast wicket, the kind of wicket on which records are broken.

Lord's, the home of the Marylebone Cricket Club (the M.C.C.), has been the centre of English cricket since the 'laws' or rules were first fixed at the end of the eighteenth century, and it is still one of the most famous cricket grounds in the world. Wherever the English have gone—Australia, Africa, India, New Zealand, the West Indies, Pakistan—they have taken the game of cricket with them. And today teams come from these parts of the British Commonwealth to play against England on this ground where cricket has been played for one hundred and fifty years.

This was the first day of the Second Test Match against Australia. The First Test had been played at Nottingham and the other three of the series would be at Manchester, Leeds, and the Oval, London's other famous cricket ground. Except for a short break for lunch, David and his father had sat here all day. It had been very hot, but now the afternoon sun was low in the sky and there was a gentle wind to stir the handkerchiefs that people had put on their heads in the mid-day heat.

The Australians had been batting all day—and batting well. For hour after hour the English bowlers had worked away at them, but with little success. The wicket was perfect and the Australian batsmen had been hitting the ball all over the ground. It was not a record Test Match innings—like the 903 runs for seven wickets made by England at the Oval in 1938—but by the time the last wicket fell the visitors had scored 439. Now, with an hour left before the close of play, the crowd were hoping to see England make a good start.

David and his father watched the Australian team come out on to the field. England's two opening batsmen followed, each carrying his bat under his arm. The Australian fast bowler walked back from the wicket, turned and ran quickly up to bowl. It was a ball that every batsman dreams about. The sound of the ball on the bat could be heard all over the ground, and the crowd shouted as the ball flew over the boundary. The umpire signalled a six and the batsman, who had started to run, walked back to his wicket, smiling in reply to the cheers of the crowd. Six from the first ball of the innings and the wicket still perfect: this was going to be a match to remember.

* * * * *

Three-quarters of an hour later, when stumps were drawn, the opening batsmen were still at the wicket and the score stood at 63. Mr Brown and David, like a good many other people in the great crowd, were looking forward to the next day's play. But by this time the wind was blowing quite strongly and the clouds were gathering. Rain in the night might spoil the ground; rain the following day might stop play altogether. But rain is something that can always happen in England. That is why the English enjoy a fine day so much when it does come.

CONVERSATION

(Mr Brown and his son David are at Lord's watching the Test Match)

MR BROWN: I daresay there are nicer ways of spending a fine afternoon than watching cricket, but I can't think of one.

DAVID: If the cricket is good. Otherwise I'd sooner play.

MR BROWN: Yes, I suppose so. But when you get to my age you'll be glad to sit and watch—Oh, look at that! Well played, sir! Did you see how he just touched that ball as it went by him and helped it on its way?

DAVID: The Australians are playing well, but I don't think they'll break any records today. It looks as if they'll be

all out by tea-time, so that England will have a chance
to go in before close of play.

MR BROWN: Let's hope so. No, there'll be no records broken
today. Not like the day when . . .

DAVID: I know, I know—when you saw Donald Bradman
help to make 451 runs at the Oval in 1934.

MR BROWN: You can laugh, but you could see real cricket
in those days. I shall never forget the day when England
finished their record innings of 903 for seven wickets in
1938. That was at the Oval, too. How the crowd
cheered! But the batsman I enjoyed watching most was
Jack Hobbs. Hobbs seemed to be able to make centuries
without any trouble at all. When he was playing at his
best it was something to remember.

*(An old man sitting next to them has been listening to what they
have been saying. Now he can keep quiet no longer)*

OLD MAN *(to Mr Brown)*: Excuse me, my name's Jackson.
I couldn't help hearing what you were saying. You're
right, you know.

MR BROWN: Am I? Right about what?

MR JACKSON: About Hobbs. He was the greatest cricketer,
but I've seen other great cricketers.

MR BROWN: Who are you thinking of?

MR JACKSON: C. B. Fry. He was the perfect batsman. The
most beautiful performance—every movement just
right. He could do what he liked with the bowling. Yes,
those were the days!

MR BROWN: There you are, David. I tell you that cricket
today is no better than it was thirty years ago, and here's
Mr Jackson telling me that it was as good fifty years
ago. Soon we shall start playing the favourite game of
cricket-lovers.

DAVID: What's that?

MR BROWN: Making up a team drawn from the best cricketers of all time; I wonder if anyone from today's match would find a place in our team?

MR JACKSON: I don't think so. Oh, well bowled! Took the middle stump clean out of the ground. Well, that's the end of their innings—439. We ought to do better than that tomorrow if the wicket and the weather hold. Now for some tea.

DAVID: A jolly good idea. I'm hungry—and thirsty, too.

SENTENCE PATTERNS

56.   Perfect Continuous Tenses

(a) Present Perfect Continuous

This tense is used to show that something has been going on for some time and is still going on now or has just stopped. Notice that the Present Perfect looks back at the past from the present moment, but the action is thought of as finished; with the Present Perfect Continuous, we are interested in the time while the action was going on.

He has been living here for ten years (and still lives here).

He has been working all the morning (and is still working).

I have been waiting for the bus for half an hour (and I am still waiting).

Susan has been working for Mr Robinson for a year (and is still working).

Mr Brown has been staying with some friends in Scotland (and is still staying).

I have been thinking about the question you asked me (and I am still thinking).

It has been raining all the morning.

I have been looking for him everywhere.

(b) Past Perfect Continuous

This tense is used to show that something continued to happen until some point of time in the past and was still happening at that point.

They had been batting all day (and were still batting).
He had been working for three hours (and was still working).
It had been raining all the morning (and was still raining).
I had been waiting for her to arrive (and was still waiting).
We had been staying with our friends in Italy (and were still staying).
I had been reading an interesting book (and was still reading).
He had been learning English for three years (and was still learning).
She had been sitting in the sunshine, watching the sea (and was still watching).
We had been sleeping for about an hour (and were still sleeping).
The man had been driving since early morning (and was still driving).

57.   Prepositions after Certain Verbs

To

She gave the book to her friend.
He promised the money to his brother.
He sold the house to a friend.
Susan showed the letter to the Manager.

Other verbs followed by *to* are:

do (something to someone), *explain, lend, pay, read, send, write, belong, happen, listen.*

For

Susan chose a present for her brother.
I bought some flowers for Mrs Brown.

Mr Brown is getting some vegetables for dinner.
I am keeping this seat for a friend.
Will you order some coffee for me, please?

Other verbs followed by *for* are: *buy, cook, do* (something for someone), *fetch, find, get, leave, make, order, save, write, arrange.*

From

Have you heard from your friend lately?
Where did you get it from?

On

She spends all her money on clothes.
Are you sure I can rely on him?
Have they agreed on what they will do?

With

They are living with her parents until their own house is ready.
He is in bed with a bad cold.
He speaks with a good English accent.

58.   Phrasal Verbs—*Look*

Look after

Will you look after the dog while I'm in the shop?
We are looking after the house while they're away.
Look after that book—it's valuable.

Look at

What is she looking at?
She is looking at the hats in the shop window.
A cat may look at a king.

Look for

He's looking for the pen he lost yesterday.
It's like looking for a needle in a haystack.

I'm afraid he's looking for trouble.
We've been looking for you everywhere.

Look out

The children sat in the corner of the railway carriage, because they wanted to look out of the window.
Look out! You'll get run over.
You'll get into trouble if you don't look out.

Look round

She looked round when I called her name.
In most of the big stores you can walk in and look round without having to buy.

Look up

He didn't even look up from his book when I came into the room.
I looked up his number in the telephone book.

59. The uses of *So*

(a) In short answers, agreeing with what has been said:

Is he arriving today? (Yes) I think so.
Will it be fine tomorrow? I hope so.
They are moving to London, aren't they? (Yes) I've heard so.
Have they sold their house? I believe so.

(b) To intensify or emphasise an adjective or adverb:

I didn't think I was so tired.
This car is so easy to drive.
It was so nice to see you again.
We didn't expect it to be so cold.
It is always so quiet in the country.
I didn't think I would get there so quickly.
She always dresses so smartly.
I wish they didn't come to see us so often.

Does he always shout so loudly?
I like this coal; it burns so brightly.

(c) To introduce a clause of result:
He was so tired that he fell asleep.
It was so warm that I opened the windows.
The room was so crowded that we could hardly breathe.
It was so wet that we had to stay in all day.

(d) In short phrases replacing a complete statement with *also:*
Tom likes going to the theatre, and so do I.
Mary went to London yesterday, and so did John.
"You ought to be more careful." "And so ought you."
"I must go to bed early." "And so must I."

NEW WORDS

accent ('aksənt)
bat (bat)
    batsman ('batsmən)
boundary ('baundri)
bowler ('boulə)
cloud (klaud)
haystack ('heistak)
innings ('iniŋz)
movement ('muːvmənt)
needle ('niːdl)
preparation ('prepə'reiʃn)
run (*noun*) (rʌn)
stump (stʌmp)
success (sək'ses)
umpire ('ʌmpaiə)
wicket ('wikit)

bowl, bowled (boul, bould)
cheer, cheered (tʃiə, tʃiəd)
draw, drew, drawn (droː, druː, droːn)
dream, dreamed (dreamt) (driːm, driːmd, dremt)
fix, fixed (fiks, fikst)
gather, gathered ('gaðə, 'gaðəd)
signal, signalled ('signl, 'signld)
spoil, spoiled (spoil, spoild)
stir, stirred (stəː, stəːd)
touch, touched (tʌtʃ, tʌtʃt)
understand, understood ('ʌndə'stand, 'ʌndə'stud)

bat, batted (bat, 'batid)

against (ə'geinst)

altogether ('ɔːltə'geðə)   otherwise (' ʌðəwaiz)
flat (flæt)   perfect ('pəɪfikt)
gentle ('dʒentl)   valuable ('valjəbl)
jolly ('dʒɔli)

Idioms

at its best (ət its 'best)
the close of play (ðə 'klouz əv 'plei)
to make a good start (tə 'meik ə gud 'staɪt)
a good many people (ə 'gud meni 'piːpl)
Those were the days! ('ðouz wə ðə 'deiz)
if the weather holds (if ðə 'weðə 'houldz)

EXERCISES

A. *Answer these questions in sentences:*

1. What is 'a fast wicket'?
2. What do the letters M.C.C. mean?
3. What other countries are there in the British Commonwealth besides those named here?
4. What is a Test Match?
5. Where in England are the five Test Matches played?
6. What is the record for a Test Match innings?
7. Why do the English enjoy a fine summer day so much?
8. Cricket is played in summer. What is the most popular
   winter sport in England?
9. How many players are there in a cricket team?
10. What does an umpire do? What is the man called who
    does this at a football match?

B. *Use these phrasal verbs in sentences other than those given in
   the Sentence Patterns:*

look for; look round; go out; go with; come across; come
round; put out; put back; take in; take up.

C. *Put the right prepositions into these sentences:*

1. He lent some money . . . his friend.
2. She told me to fetch some flowers . . . the garden.
3. I will leave some supper . . . you in the dining-room.
4. He spends far too much money . . . books.
5. He opened the door . . . a key . . . his pocket.
6. This house belongs . . . my father.
7. Mrs Brown was cooking a meal . . . the family.
8. They travelled North . . . London . . . Edinburgh . . . train.
9. I wrote the letter . . . a pen which I took . . . the desk . . . the sitting-room.
10. I met her . . . the boat coming . . . France.

D. *Replace the masculine nouns and pronouns in these sentences by the feminine forms:*

1. He was a very kind husband and father.
2. The actor was playing the part of a waiter.
3. The king was ill, but he refused to see a doctor.
4. Mr Smith's son is at a boys' school in London.

E. *Put the verbs in these sentences into the Perfect Continuous Tense:*

1. It was raining all the morning.
2. We are staying with some friends in the country.
3. They will be trying to learn English.
4. The Australian team were batting for three hours.
5. He is thinking of buying a new house.
6. He will be working here for three weeks.
7. I shall wait for you for half an hour.
8. He was acting in a play at a London theatre.
9. He will cut the grass in the garden.
10. They are looking for a new house in Bishopton.

F. *Put the missing possessives into these sentences:*

1. You say this is . . . book; it really belongs to a friend of . . .
2. Susan said . . . brother had passed . . . examination.
3. There are . . . coats. You take . . . and I'll take . . .
4. This dog has hurt . . . leg.
5. Tom has no ink in . . . pen. Have you any in . . .?
6. He is always losing . . . pencils. I have lent him two of . . . already, and the one he is now using is really . . ., although he says it is . . .
7. I have left . . . umbrella in . . . room. Will you lend me . . .?
8. I will get . . . ticket for you. Susan is with . . . boy-friend, so he will get . . .
9. Mr and Mrs Brown invited us to . . . house, and there we met a cousin of . . .
10. He's not a friend of . . ., although I've met him at . . . brother's house once or twice.

G. *Use the following words in a continuous composition. You may use the words in any order you wish:*

understand; island; count; cry; meeting; amuse.

H. *Write these sentences first in the negative and then as questions:*

1. He plays a game of cricket every week-end.
2. He scored fifteen runs in fifteen minutes.
3. David often goes to Lord's with his father.
4. He ought to give his passport to the customs officer.
5. You can go on shore without a landing card.
6. They show visitors round the Houses of Parliament.
7. He does his homework every evening.
8. He should listen to what his brother says.
9. They counted the votes at the end of the debate.
10. Tom bought Susan a very expensive ring.

I. *Write short responses agreeing with the following:*

1. It's a lovely day today.
2. She didn't stay very long.
3. We shall have a nice summer this year.
4. We needn't go yet, need we?
5. You've lost a handkerchief from your pocket.
6. Mr Brown works in London.
7. That player batted very well.
8. We mustn't cross the road here.
9. You've never been here before, have you?

J. *Respond to the following, using* think, hope, believe, *or* am afraid, *with* so *or* not:

1. Have you lost your ticket?
2. Tom has bought a new car.
3. It'll rain before we get home.
4. He won't catch that bus.
5. There is a new headmaster at David's school, isn't there?
6. I expect you'll pass your examination.
7. Can't he afford to buy a book for himself?
8. Will you be away for more than a week?
9. Will you be going to Scotland for your holiday?
10. Must you go home so soon?

K. *Put the word* who, which, what, where, why, *or* how, *into these sentences:*

1. He did not know . . . had happened.
2. Do you know . . . to go?
3. He showed them . . . bus to take.
4. We never found out . . . the window was broken.
5. I have decided . . . to invite to the party.
6. Susan told me . . . her friend lived.
7. The teacher asked David . . . he was always late.
8. I will teach you . . . to cook.
9. He told the waitress . . . he had had for his tea.
10. Have you heard . . . he has gone for his holiday?

L. *Put a pronoun as indirect object into the blank space in each of these sentences:*

1. The jeweller sold . . . a ring.
2. The bookmaker gave . . . the money we had won.
3. He told . . . the answer to the question she had asked.
4. The assistant found . . . the books they were looking for.
5. I will show . . . the picture and then you can decide whether you want to buy it.
6. "Mr Thompson taught . . . English when I was at school," said David.
7. The policeman asked . . . several questions, but they couldn't tell him anything.
8. A friend lent . . . some money, but we have spent it all.
9. We saved . . . a seat, but she missed the train.
10. They refused . . . a room at the hotel, so he had to go elsewhere.

M. *Put the word* can, must, ought, *or* may *into the blank space in each of these sentences:*

1. Anyone . . . learn English if he tries hard enough.
2. He . . . be at the races this afternoon.
3. You . . . to have central heating in your house.
4. Passengers . . . show their passports on landing.
5. You . . . drive on the left side of the road in England.
6. . . . you play the piano?
7. "You . . . have a half-day holiday today," said the manager.
8. It . . . rain tomorrow, but I hope it won't.
9. Customers . . . to count their change before they leave a shop.
10. In England parents . . . send their children to school.

N. *Put the word* much, many, more, less, *or* fewer *into the blank spaces in these sentences:*

1. Because it rained all day, there were . . . people at the Derby this year than usual.

2. If he had . . . money Tom would buy Susan a . . . expensive ring.

3. How . . . runs has this batsman scored?

4. Susan didn't have . . . difficulty in finding the ring she wanted.

5. There is . . . noise in the house when David is at school.

6. . . . people in England enjoy going to the races.

7. Now that so . . . people have cars, . . . people travel by bus.

8. We'd better hurry, as we haven't . . . time.

9. When a man gets married he has . . . money to spend on clothes.

10. There was so . . . noise that we couldn't hear ourselves speak.

O. *Write a short conversation between yourself (or someone else from your country) and an Englishman about cricket.*

Phrasal Verb

A visitor to England, who did not know English very well, was travelling with a friend by train. He was leaning out of the window and his friend saw he might get hurt.

"Look out!" he shouted.

The visitor leaned farther out of the train, and was nearly hit by a tree at the side of the railway line. He turned to his friend and said angrily,

"Why do you say 'Look out' when you mean 'Look in'?"

farther ('faɪðə)

LESSON 16

The Browns Give a Dinner-party

THIS evening the Browns have invited some friends to dinner. Their house is not very big, so when they want to invite a large number of friends they have a sherry party; then people stand about talking, and a lot of people can get into one room. But today it is just a small dinner-party for four of their friends: Mr and Mrs Carter and Mr and Mrs Macdonald.

Henry Carter is the manager of the factory where Susan's fiancé, Tom Smith, works. His wife, Dorothy, often goes shopping with Mrs Brown. Ian Macdonald lives in Edinburgh; he was very kind during Mr Brown's visit to Edinburgh a few months ago. He and his wife Jean are on holiday in London, so the Browns are glad to be able to return some of their kindness. Susan and David are not at home this evening: Susan has gone to the theatre with Tom Smith, and David is at the cinema.

The guests arrive at about half past seven and are shown into the sitting-room where Mr Brown pours drinks for them. Sherry is the most popular wine in England; men usually prefer dry sherry, but women often prefer sweet. At eight o'clock Mrs Brown says that dinner is ready, and they move into the dining-room.

Mary Brown does all the cooking in her house, but when she has a dinner-party she is helped by Mrs Higgins, the woman who comes in to help her with the housework each day; the Browns do not have a servant living in the house. The Browns' dinner-parties are not very formal, but the food and wine are good and the cooking is excellent. There are usually four courses: soup (or, in the summer, fruit juice), fish, meat (beef, mutton, or more often, chicken, or duck), and a sweet; the sweet may be pudding or tart, or perhaps ice-cream. Cheese and biscuits and coffee are served after the sweet, and there are different kinds of fruit also on the table. Wine (either red or white) is drunk with the meal and brandy with the coffee.

Mrs Brown is always a little worried in case something goes wrong, but this evening everything goes well and the guests make many kind remarks about her good cooking.

The conversation at table is lively and interesting. Mrs Brown will not let the men talk about trade, banking or politics all the time; when she thinks anyone is getting tired, she changes the subject. She is very good at getting people to talk in an interesting way, and there is always plenty of gaiety and laughter at her dinner-table. Mr Brown often wonders how his wife can manage to make sure that all her guests are enjoying themselves, and at the same time see that the dinner is being well served. But then, he has known for a long time that his wife is a very clever woman!

When dinner is over the party return to the sitting-room. For a while the ladies sit and talk while the men stand about smoking their cigars and perhaps 'talking business'. Presently, Mr Brown brings out some new records he thinks his guests will like to hear, and puts them on the record-player. Or he will show them a film of one of their holidays. Both Mr and Mrs Brown sing rather well, and sometimes they entertain their guests in this way.

At about eleven on this evening the Macdonalds decide they must go, as they have to get back to London, where they are staying with friends. The Carters offer to run them to Bishopton station in their car. So after a final drink (whisky for the men and sherry for the ladies) all the guests leave together. Mr and Mrs Brown see them off at the garden gate. The guests thank their host and hostess for a pleasant evening, and drive off. The Browns go back into the house for a last little talk by the fire before going to bed.

CONVERSATION

(*Ian and Jean Macdonald arrive at the Browns' house. Henry Carter and his wife Dorothy are already there*)

MRS BROWN: Hello. How are you? Do come in. I've heard so much about you both from my husband.

MR MACDONALD. We're always pleased to see John in Edinburgh. Ah, here he is. Hello, John. Nice to see you.

MR BROWN: Nice to see you, too. Mary, this is Ian and Jean Macdonald—but I see you've already introduced yourselves. Come along in.

(*They go into the sitting-room*)

MR BROWN: Henry, Dorothy, I want you to meet two very good friends of mine, Ian and Jean Macdonald. Jean, Ian—Henry and Dorothy Carter. Now let me get you a drink: Sherry, whisky? Jean?

MRS MACDONALD: Sherry, please.

MR BROWN: Sweet or dry?

MRS MACDONALD: Sweet, please.

MR BROWN: I don't have to ask a Scotsman what he will drink. Whisky?

MR MACDONALD: As a matter of fact, I'd rather have sherry, please. Dry.

MR CARTER: Do you often come down to London?

MR MACDONALD: No, I'm sorry to say we don't. Both Jean and I like London, but Edinburgh's a capital city, you know, and we manage most of our own affairs these days. We usually get away to the Highlands for our holidays instead of coming south.

MRS CARTER: How long are you staying?

MRS MACDONALD: For about another week. And as a matter of fact I shall be quite glad to get back. I always find London very tiring—there is so much rushing about from place to place. People seldom seem to stay still for a moment.

MRS BROWN: Even those who *live* in London often feel like that. That's why we're pleased we live a good way out.

(Later—after dinner)

MR BROWN: I don't know if Ian can advise you, Henry. I believe your company is looking for a position for a new factory in Scotland.

MR CARTER: Yes. We have a factory here and one near Birmingham. We think it is better to divide the work among several small factories in different places rather than to have it all in one large one.

Mr Macdonald: Yes, I'm sure I can help. There are many towns in Scotland which would be glad to have a factory bringing more work. What do you make?

Mr Carter: Bicycles. At present we buy all the parts made of rubber—tyres and so on—but now we should like to make these ourselves.

Mr Macdonald: Wait a moment. I think I know just the thing for you. One of our customers at the Bank has a factory for sale not very far from Edinburgh. He makes rubber heels for shoes.

Mr Carter: That sounds just what we want. And rubber too. I'd like to know more about it.

Mr Macdonald: Why not come up to Edinburgh and see for yourself? I'll be glad to arrange this with our customer.

Mr Brown: There you are, Henry. You see how useful it is to know a bank manager or two. Now I wonder if you'd like to hear these new records we bought the other day.

. . . . .

Mrs Macdonald: Well, I really think we must go now. We don't want to be too late back in case the friends we are staying with wait up for us.

Mr Carter: We're going now, too, so we'll run you down to the station.

Mr Macdonald: That's very kind of you.

Mrs Macdonald: Thank you, Mary, for a lovely evening. We *have* enjoyed it.

Mrs Brown: Thank you for coming. We look forward to seeing you again when you're next in London.

Mr Macdonald: We hope to see you in Edinburgh before then. John promised you would spend a holiday in the Highlands with us before long.

Mr Carter: Good-night, John. Good-night, Mary. Thank

you for a very nice evening. Your cooking was excellent,
Mary, as it always is. Give my good wishes to Susan.
Her Tom is doing very well indeed at the factory, by
the way.

MR BROWN: Good. Thanks for taking Jean and Ian to the
station. Good-night.

SENTENCE PATTERNS

60. *Get*

There are many uses of *get*:

(*a*) As a simple verb it can mean:

  (i) *fetch, buy, obtain, find*

    Where did you get that book?
    She went to get a handkerchief from her bedroom.
    I got a new coat when I was in London.
    Get me another cup of tea, please.
    He got a new tyre for his bicycle.
    Where did the dog get that bone?
    You can't get fresh strawberries at this time of the year.

  (ii) *receive*

    Did you get my letter last week?
    Tom got a surprise when he opened the parcel.
    The children get a holiday if they work well.
    You won't get your pocket money if you're rude.
    You'll get your dinner as soon as it's ready.
    How much money does Susan get each week?

  (iii) *become*

    He got tired of waiting and went home.
    You will get used to English coffee in time.
    He has been ill, but is getting well again now.
    We need less sleep as we get older.

You'll be late if you don't get ready now.

Susan and Tom are getting married next year.

The days are getting longer and the weather is getting warmer.

(iv) *arrive at*

When we got to the station, the train had gone.

You'll never get there if you don't hurry.

David gets to school at about nine o'clock.

What time do we get to London?

What time does the boat get in?

(b) *Get* is used with *have* especially in conversation, although the use of *have* without *got* is also common.

(i) For possession:

What have you (got) there?

I've (got) a new bell for my bicycle.

Has she (got) any money?

We hadn't (got) time to stop and talk.

I've (got) a brother and two sisters.

How many children has your sister (got)?

(ii) For obligation:

I've got to be home by eleven.

We've got to call at the chemist's on our way home.

Have you got to go now?

You haven't got to do this if you don't want to.

I've got to go to Birmingham next week.

(c) *Get* as a phrasal verb:

With *get* as a phrasal verb there is usually some suggestion of difficulty.

Get at

She put the sweets on a high shelf where the children couldn't get at them.

P.E. II – 16

They wanted a quiet holiday, so they took a cottage in the country where no one could get at them.

He spoke so little English that we couldn't get at his meaning.

Get away

He was caught by the police, but he managed to get away.

We like to get away for a holiday now and then, without the children.

Get back

He has gone to London for a few days, but he hopes to get back before Friday.

He swam a long way from the shore, and then found he couldn't get back.

Get down

He had climbed on top of the cupboard, but when someone took the chair away he couldn't get down.

He read the dictation passage so quickly that the students couldn't get it down.

Get in

He stopped the car and invited his friend to get in.

David wants to go to a university, but he doesn't know whether he'll get in.

This train is supposed to get in at seven thirty-five.

Get into

If you try to bring watches through the customs without paying duty you'll get into trouble.

He has grown so much that he can hardly get into his clothes.

Get off

Get off the bus at the next stop.

You will have to brush your shoes hard to get the dirt off.

Get on

You will have to work hard if you want to get on.
She doesn't get on very well with her sister.
How are they getting on?

Get out

He got out the car and they went for a drive.
How much money did she get out of him?
As the car would not go, she decided to get out and walk.
We shall go to the party if we can't get out of it.

Get over

Has he got over his illness yet?
A new job is always difficult, but once you get over the first
    week, you'll be all right.

Get up

I never get up in the morning very early.
They are getting up a party to go to the theatre.
She had got herself up in a brightly coloured dress and hat.

61.   Words as Different Parts of Speech

Some words are used as more than one part of speech.

(*a*) Nouns and verbs

We have had a lot of *rain* this summer.
Will it *rain* again today?

They saw a *light* in the window.
Will you *light* the fire, please?

My wife needs some *help* in the house.
Will you *help* me to pick these flowers?

He has cut his *hand*.
Hand me that book, please.

Other words used as nouns and verbs are:

*ache, act, answer, bat, bet, bite, book, brush, care, change,
climb, comb, cook, copy, cough, cover, cut, dance, dress, drink,
drive, dust, fall, fight, guide, iron, judge, jump, kick, kiss, laugh,
lift, look, need, offer, oil, paint, photograph, pity, place, plan,
plant, polish, race, rest, shave, show, sleep, smell, smile, smoke,
snow, start, step, stop, store, swim, swing, switch, taste, touch,
use, vote, walk, watch, wish, work.*

(b) Adjectives and verbs

The door's *shut*.
Please *shut* the door.

Your glass is *empty*.
He was told to *empty* his pockets on the table.

He took a *clean* handkerchief from his pocket.
Clean your shoes before you come in from the garden.

Other words used as adjectives and verbs are:

*admired, advertised, beaten, clear, cut, determined, dirty,
disappointed, drawn, free, frozen, haunted, hurt, light, live,
married, mixed, packed, retired, satisfied, separate, shut, signed,
spoiled, twisted, used, warm, wet.*

62. Position of Adverbs

(a) The usual position of adverbs in English is at the end of the
sentence. When more than one adverb is used, they are placed
in this order:

Manner, Place, Time

He worked hard at school this morning.
I cannot work well in the afternoon.
They arrived home at midnight.
They lived happily ever after.
He lives quietly in the country.

(*b*) Time adverbs are often placed at the beginning of the sentence, particularly if there are several adverbs in the sentence:

Soon he will be travelling regularly to London every day.
After lunch they sat quietly in deck-chairs in the garden.
Yesterday they walked steadily for twenty miles towards London.
Before lunch the children went quietly to the bathroom to wash their hands.
This time last year we were sitting lazily in the sunshine in the south of France.

There are some other adverbs which are often placed before the main verb in this way.
The most important are:

almost, already, ever, hardly, just, nearly, quite, scarcely.

We had almost reached the top of the mountain.
Have you ever seen him before?
They had hardly started when it began to rain.
I have just finished reading this book.
Have you quite made up your mind to go?
She was nearly killed when she fell downstairs.

63.   Position of Adverbials

An adverbial such as *on, off, up* is added to many verbs to give them a special meaning (see Phrasal Verbs, Sentence Pattern No. 51, page 192).
Where the verb is followed by a noun or pronoun as object and an adverbial, the adverbial sometimes comes before the object and sometimes after.

(a) *Adverbials before the object*

Where the object is long or of special importance in the sentence, the adverbial is placed before it.

He gave up a good job in the factory.
Take off your wet coat and hat.
He gave up all the money in his pocket.
He threw away everything he didn't want.
Have you found out the name of the man who took your coat?
She brought in a beautiful bunch of flowers.
He put on all the lights in the house.
The company has taken over all the old factory and part of the new.
Have you thought out the answer to my question?
She sent off a birthday present to her friend.

(b) *Adverbials after the object*

Where the object is short, or a pronoun, the adverbial is placed after it.

Take your hat off in the house.
Put these away.
I sent the letters off this morning
Hand it over.
Take it away.
Pick them up.
Who knocked him down?
They are trying to keep us out.
The thief gave himself up.
Did you pick your gloves up?

NEW WORDS

affair (ə'feə)
banking ('baŋkiŋ)
biscuit ('biskit)
bone (boun)
bunch (bʌntʃ)
collector (kə'lektə)
copy (*noun* and *verb*) ('kopi)
cottage ('kotidʒ)
course (koːs)
duck (dʌk)
duty ('djuːti)
fiancé ('fiːaːnsei)
gaiety ('geiiti)
host (houst)
  hostess ('houstis)
kick (*noun* and *verb*) (kik)
mutton ('mʌtn)
passage ('pasidʒ)
photograph (*noun* and *verb*)
  ('foutəgraːf)
polish (*noun* and *verb*) ('poliʃ)
record-player ('rekoːd 'pleiə)
sherry ('ʃeri)
smell (*noun* and *verb*) (smel)
strawberry ('stroːbri)

trade (treid)
whisky ('wiski)

admire, admired (ad'maiə,
  ad'maiəd)
advise, advised (əd'vaiz,
  əd'vaizd)
entertain, entertained
  ('entə'tein, 'entə'teind)
haunt, haunted (hoːnt,
  'hoːntid)
introduce, introduced
  ('intrə'djuːs, 'intrə'djuːst)
mix, mixed (mix, mixt)
obtain, obtained (əb'tein,
  əb'teind)
offer, offered ('ofə, 'ofəd)
retire, retired (ri'taiə,
  ri'taiəd)

formal ('foːml)
lively ('laivli)
presently ('prezəntli)
scarcely ('skeəsli)
useful ('juːsful)

Idioms

do come in ('duː kʌm 'in)
in case something goes wrong (in 'keis 'sʌmθiŋ gouz 'roŋ)
to run someone to the station (tə 'rʌn 'sʌmwʌn tə ðə 'steiʃn)
I'm sorry to say (aim 'sori tə 'sei)
just the thing ('dʒʌst ðə 'θiŋ)
to see for yourself (tə 'siː fə jə'self)

EXERCISES

A. *Answer these questions in sentences:*

1. What do English people usually drink before dinner?
2. What do Scotsmen usually like to drink?
3. What two kinds of sherry are there?
4. How do the Browns entertain their guests after dinner?
5. What did Mr Carter ask Mr Macdonald about?
6. What does Mr Carter's factory make?
7. Give the meaning of the words *menu, course,* and *sweet.*
8. How many courses are there usually at a small dinner-party in England?
9. How does Mrs Brown make sure that the conversation at her dinner-table is lively and interesting?
10. Why did the Carters and the Macdonalds leave together?

B. *Put the adverbs and adverbial phrases in brackets into the right places in these sentences:*

1. They have lived (*for the past ten years*) (*by themselves*) (*quietly*) (*in the country*).
2. He worked (*in his room*) (*hard*) (*all day yesterday*).
3. We have our meals (*often*) (*in summer*) (*in the garden*).
4. We had finished our work (*almost*) (*by midday*).
5. He works (*sometimes*) (*hard*) (*all day*).
6. They stayed (*in their hotel*) (*quietly*) (*yesterday*).
7. We are tired (*by the end of the day*) (*usually*).
8. The wind blew (*all night*) (*coldly*).
9. The children run (*happily*) (*to school*) (*every day*).
10. He has spoken (*just*) (*to his mother*) (*rudely*).

C. *Use these phrasal verbs in sentences different from those given in the Sentence Patterns:*

to get on; to get out; to look on; to look after; to go out; to come out; to come down; to put off; to take on.

D. *Write sentences using each of the following words first as a noun, then as a verb:*

answer; book; brush; change; cook; cover; dress; smile; smoke.

E. *Put the adverbials into the right place in these sentences:*

   1. He gave all the money that he had in his pockets (*away*).
   2. I sent the parcel this afternoon (*off*).
   3. Whatever happens you must help these people (*out*).
   4. If the dog is noisy we shall put him in the garden (*out*).
   5. Have they taken their new house yet? (*over*).
   6. Pick all the toys and books from the carpet (*up*).
   7. That child is making too much noise; take him (*away*).
   8. He put his hat and coat and shoes (*on*).
   9. He gave the ticket to the collector at the station (*up*).
   10. You should think this a little more carefully before you decide what to do (*out*).

F. *Write sentences using each of the following words, first as an adjective, then as a verb:*

clear; dirty; dry; shut; warm; cut; light; empty; clean.

G. *Write ten sentences each containing an adjective of colour.*

H. *Put the missing -self pronouns into the right place in these sentences:*

   1. He cut with a knife.
   2. I haven't a car, but I often drive my friend's car.
   3. I found the only person there who could not speak English.
   4. You must do this if you want it done well.
   5. The house is quite small but there is a large garden.
   6. She will be quite safe; she can look after.
   7. He has washed, but his shoes are very dirty.

8. You must finish this work; I haven't time to help you.
9. Did he hurt when he fell off the wall?
10. Are you going to use this or give it to your friend?

I. *Write imperative sentences using the following ideas and putting the adverbials at the end:*

Picking up a book—Pick that book up!

Putting out the light; putting on your hat; pulling up your socks; turning off the light; pouring out the wine; taking off your coat; tidying up your bedroom; putting down those books; throwing away the empty boxes; taking your friends out to dinner.

J. *Put the verbs in this passage into the correct Past Tense:*

This (*be*) Edouard's first visit to England. He (*look forward*) to coming for a long time and now he (*be*) on the steamer which (*cross*) the Channel. On the journey from Paris he (*talk*) to a man he (*meet*) on the train, and now they both (*watch*) the English coast coming nearer and nearer. The sun (*shine*) and the white cliffs (*look*) clean and bright. He (*not see*) the fog and rain that his friends (*tell*) him always (*hang*) over England. Near them (*be*) an English family who (*come*) home from Italy where they (*live*) for a long time. The father (*work*) for an English firm that (*have*) customers in Italy. The family (*stop*) in Paris for a short holiday on their way home. They (*say*) that some friends (*meet*) them at Dover.

"Well, we (*arrive*)," Edouard's friend (*say*) as the boat (*stop*) beside the quay and the passengers (*begin*) to go ashore. "It (*be*) a very pleasant journey. Thank you, and good-bye." The man (*lift*) his hat politely and (*go*) off to see about his luggage. When Edouard (*find*) a porter he, too, (*go*) ashore. He (*be*) in England at last.

K. *Finish these sentences with clauses beginning* if *or* unless:

1. I shall go to the party . . .
2. They would learn English more quickly . . .

3. Mr Brown does not like going to the seaside . . .
4. . . . you will be late.
5. . . . I should be very angry.
6. They would go to Spain for a holiday . . .
7. We shan't go out today . . .
8. . . . I should give some to my friends.
9. We always turn off the television . . .
10. Their garden would look much tidier . . .

L. *Write a composition about a visit you paid to a friend's house.*

Home Comfort

A story is told about Sheridan, the writer, who lived one hundred and fifty years ago.

Drury Lane Theatre in London belonged to him, and one day it was burned down. During the fire some friends found him sitting in his house looking through the window at the burning theatre.

"How can you sit there like that," they asked, "while your theatre is burning down and all your money will be lost?"

"Well," said Sheridan calmly, "it's a pity if a man can't sit quietly at home by his own fire-side."

comfort ('kʌmfət)

LESSON 17

New Year's Eve

IT is New Year's Eve. As the hands of the clock move towards midnight the old year is slowly dying; in a few minutes now the New Year will be born. It is a time for looking back—and looking forward. We look back over all that has happened during the past year, to ourselves, to our country and to the world. We look forward with hope to the New Year that is just beginning—hope that it will bring health and happiness to those we love, and peace and goodwill to all mankind.

In Scotland the last day of the year (or *hogmanay* as the Scots call it) is the most important holiday of the winter—more important even than Christmas. On New Year's Eve friends and neighbours go about from house to house drinking a toast to the New Year in good Scotch whisky and wishing each other luck. On New Year's Day all the shops and factories are closed and families meet together for a big meal and a family party. Scottish people who live away from their home country are even more careful to keep *hogmanay* than those at home. The Scots in London, for example, meet on New Year's Eve in Piccadilly Circus in the West End or outside St Paul's Cathedral in the City and dance in the street, sing songs and, of course, drink whisky!

In England and Wales New Year's Day is not a holiday and people go to work as usual. But on New Year's Eve most people sit up till after midnight 'to see the New Year in' and many go to parties and dances. Most of the big London hotels have a New Year's Eve dance, and the Brown family are at one of these tonight.

The large room where the dance is held is beautifully decorated to look gay and exciting. There is a famous dance band on a raised platform at one end, and around the edge of the dance-floor there are little tables where people may sit when they are not dancing.

Many of the guests are 'in fancy dress': some look like well-known people of the past or present; others are in foreign clothes or the dress worn by characters from books. Prizes are given for the best ideas, and some of the dresses are very clever.

As the clock strikes midnight hundreds of coloured balloons come down from the roof, and the dancers shout, blow whistles and make a great noise to welcome in the New Year. Then all join hands to sing *Auld Lang Syne*. The New Year has begun.

CONVERSATION

(The Brown family are sitting at a table at the side of the dance-floor. It is nearly midnight)

MRS BROWN: Well, it's been quite an evening. That last dance was nearly too much for me, David. I'm getting to the age when I prefer a nice quiet dance with your father.

SUSAN: A nice quiet dance with father, indeed! You should have seen him just now, spinning round and round with Helen, like someone half his age.

MR BROWN: Well, Susan—!

SUSAN: I know, Father, I know. If I can do as well when I'm your age, you'll be surprised. That's what you were going to say, wasn't it?

MR BROWN: It was! Besides, the exercise is good for me.

MRS BROWN: Look, it's nearly midnight. Any minute now they'll be playing *Auld Lang Syne* and it'll be the New Year. We ought to look back over the year and think of all the things we've done.

DAVID: What a terrible thought!

SUSAN: Oh, Mother, don't!

MRS BROWN: Well, David, perhaps we haven't all got so many things to be ashamed of as you have. And, Susan, I may be old-fashioned, but why shouldn't I say what I like sometimes? Have you enjoyed this year?

SUSAN: Sorry, Mother. *(She takes Tom's arm)* Yes, it's been a wonderful year, hasn't it, Tom?

DAVID: Listen! There goes the first stroke of midnight. Come on everyone.

(With all the other dancers they join hands and sing Auld Lang Syne. *Back at their table, they drink a toast to the New Year)*

MR BROWN: Well, here's to the New Year, and may it be a happy one for us all—for you, David and Helen going up to the university, and for Susan and Tom with all the plans I'm sure you're making. May the future bring you happiness!

TOM: And for you and Mrs Brown, too. May you enjoy the happiness you always try to bring to others.

MRS BROWN: How kind of you, Tom. You do say the nicest things.

SUSAN: And this time, Mother, I think he really means it.

DAVID: Quick, Helen. Let's dance, before we all start crying!

(*John and Mary Brown sit watching the young people for a minute or two, then they too join the dancers. And on the table the empty glasses and burnt-out cigarettes are all that is left of another year*)

SENTENCE PATTERNS

64. *Do—Make*

Do

(*a*) *Do* means to act, perform or carry out an action:

He does his homework every evening.
Have you done anything interesting lately?
He hasn't done very well this term.
What have you done?

(*b*) *Do* has other idiomatic meanings:

Have you done yet? (finished)
How is she doing? (getting on, progressing)
Will this book do? (serve)

(*c*) *Do* is often used in place of many other verbs of action:

She is doing her hair. (brushing)
Will you do the potatoes? (clean, peel)

She was busy doing the bedrooms. (tidying)
He does the garden every Saturday. (works in)
Has Susan done all the letters yet? (typed)

Make

(a) *Make* usually means to build or produce something by using materials:

She has made a new dress.
He has made a book-shelf for his bedroom.
They have made a new road from London to Birmingham.

(b) *Make* has other idiomatic meanings:

She makes trouble wherever she goes.
He made the boys work hard.
Don't make me laugh.
He made fun of the hat she was wearing.

Do and *Make* as Phrasal Verbs

Do

Do away with

They have done away with the trams in most English towns.

Do up

Do up your shoe-lace.
Do up the buttons on your coat this cold evening.

Do with

He has been working hard lately and could do with a holiday.
We could do with a little more coal on the fire.

Do without

As she was getting fat she decided to do without bread and potatoes.

I can't do without a cigarette after meals.
You can't do without a raincoat in England.

Make

Make for

We made for the nearest house to get out of the rain.
As soon as the meeting was over everyone made for the door.
At the week-end many Londoners make for the seaside.

Make off

The man made off when the policeman appeared.
The children made off after they had broken the window.
Someone made off with their clothes while they were swimming.

Make out

I can't make out what she's trying to say.
The writing is so bad that I can't make out what it says.

Make up

She made up the whole story to explain why she was late.
If any of the money is missing, you'll have to make it up.
She made herself up carefully as she wanted to look her best.

Make up for

You'll have to work hard if you're going to make up for lost
time.
He hasn't had anything to eat all day, but he'll make up for it
now.

Make do with

We shall have to make do with what we've got.
If we haven't any coffee you'll have to make do with tea.
If you can't get a new one today you'll have to make do with
this one until tomorrow.

P.E. II – 17

65.   *How?*

Here are some more question phrases with *How . . .?*

How often?

How often does she come to London?
How often have you been to Italy?
How often does this happen?

How soon?

How soon can you come?
How soon will it be finished?
How soon did he promise to write to you?

How late?

How late will you be?
How late did you come in last night?
How late does the last bus run?

How far?

How far have you walked today?
How far is London from Birmingham?
How far is it to the nearest telephone?
How far have you got with your reading?

How near?

How near is the station?
How near is the next town?
How near was your car to the one in front?

How long?

How long have you been here?
How long are you staying in England?
How long will you be before you've finished?

How long ago?

How long ago did this king live?
How long ago did you last see him?
How long ago did you first visit England?

Other question phrases with *How . . .?* are:

How old?   How much?   How many?

66.   *See, Look, Hear, Listen*

(*a*) *See—look*

We *see* whatever is in front of our eyes.
If we *look*, we take notice of what we see.

My eyes are closed, so I can't see anything.
Birds can see farther than men can.
It was so dark we couldn't see where we were going.
We looked everywhere, but we couldn't find the money.
We looked at the picture, but we didn't know who it was.
Look! Tom's driving a new car.
She looked on the shelves, but she couldn't see the book she
    wanted.
You will see the mistake if you look carefully.

See also means *to understand*

Do you see what he means?
She wasn't very clever, so she didn't see the joke.
I don't see why he wants to go abroad for his holidays.

To meet

I shall see him in London next week.
We didn't see anyone we knew at the party.
I don't see him very often.

Look also means *to appear, seem*

She doesn't look very well this morning.
It looks like rain today.
That coat looks very nice on you.

(b) Hear—listen

We *hear* whatever sound reaches our ears.
We *listen* to what interests us or holds our attention.

I can't hear anything.
He came into the room so quietly that no one heard him.
It was so quiet you could have heard a pin drop.
They like to listen to music in the evening.
You will not learn if you do not listen.
Don't listen to him; he's not telling the truth.
We heard someone talking but we didn't listen to what he
    said.
If you listen carefully you can hear the sea from here.

67.   *Else*

(a) *Else* is used with *someone, something, anyone, anything, no one, nothing* instead of a phrase with *other*.

Someone else (some other person) can do this.
I'll give you something else (some other thing) as well.
Is anyone else (any other person) coming?
Have you anything else (any other thing) to tell me?
No one else (no other person) has been here.
Nothing else (no other thing) has happened.

(b) *Else* is also used in the same way with the interrogatives *what? where? who?*

What else (what other thing) have you done?
What else are you taking with you?
Where else (in what other place) do they speak English?

Who else (what other people) did you meet?
Where else did you go for your holiday?

(c) *Or else* is used instead of an *if not* clause.

Hurry up. If you don't you'll miss the bus.
Hurry up, or else you'll miss the bus.

Speak more slowly. If you don't you'll make mistakes.
Speak more slowly, or else you'll make mistakes.

Look where you're going. If you don't you'll fall.
Look where you're going, or else you'll fall.

NEW WORDS

band (band)
button ('bʌtn)
luck (lʌk)
mankind (man'kaind)
neighbour ('neibə)
New Year's Eve
  ('njuː jiəz 'iːv)
peace (piːs)
pin (pin)
prize (praiz)

welcome ('welkəm)

peel, peeled (piːl, piːld)
spin, spun, spun (spin,
  spʌn, spʌn)

ashamed (ə'ʃeimd)
fancy ('fansi)
old-fashioned ('ould' faʃnd)
terrible ('teribl)
besides (bi'saidz)

Idioms

to drink a toast (tə 'driŋk ə 'toust)
to wish someone luck (tə 'wiʃ sʌmwʌn 'lʌk)
it's been quite an evening (its bin 'kwait ən 'iːvniŋ)
all that is left of ('oːl ðət iz 'left əv)
it's good for you (its 'gud fə ju)

EXERCISES

A. *Answer these questions in sentences:*

    1. What do people think about at the end of the year?
    2. What is New Year's Eve called in Scotland?
    3. What do Scotsmen in London do on New Year's Eve?
    4. What does *in fancy dress* mean?
    5. What fancy dress would you wear if you were going to a New Year's Eve Dance?
    6. What happens at a New Year Dance when the clock strikes twelve?
    7. Why does Mr Brown enjoy dancing?
    8. What does *to drink a toast* mean?
    9. Who do you think Helen is?
   10. What is the date of New Year's Eve?

B. *Write these sentences in a different way,* using else:

    1. When I saw him I thought he was some other person.
    2. Did you have any other thing for your birthday?
    3. No other person knows about this.
    4. In what other place can you buy these books?
    5. Walk slowly. If you don't, you'll fall over.
    6. Shut the window. If you don't, you'll catch a cold.
    7. You must pass your examination. No other thing matters.
    8. What other person was at the party?
    9. This doesn't belong to me: it must belong to some other person.
   10. He hasn't any other thing in his pocket.

C. *Put the word* see, look, hear, *or* listen *into each of these sentences:*

    1. If you . . . carefully at what he has written you will . . . the mistake.
    2. I . . . what he said, but I didn't . . . very carefully.
    3. We often . . . to the radio in the evening.

4. I don't . . . why she should . . . everything we say.
5. Did you . . . Mary this morning? She didn't . . . very well.
6. I can . . . the children's voices, but I can't . . . them from here. We'd better go and . . . for them.
7. I was so busy . . . at the pictures in the gallery that I didn't . . . the attendant say it was closing time.
8. When you can . . . the mountains from here we say "It . . . like rain".
9. I don't . . . him very often, but I . . . he is going to London next week.
10. She was . . . into the fire because she said she could . . . pictures there.

D. *Put* some, any, *or* ones *into these sentences:*

1. I have . . . new gloves, which I bought in Oxford Street.
2. We haven't . . . money, but we enjoy ourselves.
3. You can have . . . of these flowers, but leave me the blue . . .
4. Have you . . . large apples in your garden? We have only small . . . in ours.
5. Can you give me . . . writing-paper? I haven't . . . in my desk.
6. They have built . . . new houses in Bishopton, but the nicest . . . have all been sold.
7. Don't give him . . . more apples. He's had two big . . . already.
8. I am looking for . . . good coffee. Have you . . .?
9. We have . . . tea, but we haven't . . . coffee.
10. Do you want . . . apples? Yes, please; give me . . . eating and . . . cooking . . .

E. *Put the right form of pronoun into these sentences:*

1. Tom came with my father and (*I, me*).
2. Susan and (*I, me*) went to London together.
3. They gave the books to David and (*I, me*).

4. (*I, me*) like (*he, him*), and (*he, him*) likes (*I, me*).
5. (*We, us*) saw (*they, them*) at the station and (*we, us*) waved to (*they, them*) but (*they, them*) did not see (*we, us*).
6. The money was divided between Henry and (*I, me*).
7. Let (*we, us*) go to the theatre with (*they, them*).
8. Has (*he, him*) had any letters from (*they, them*)?
9. Tom hasn't a car, so I took David and (*he, him*) to the station.
10. My sister and (*I, me*) know (*they, them*) well.

F. *Put these phrases into the possessive form without* of:

1. The books of the children.
2. The school of the girls.
3. The bicycle of Charles.
4. The coat of my brother David.
5. The horse of King James.
6. The shoes of the ladies.
7. The father of Susan and David.
8. The boots of the policemen.
9. The house of the Browns.
10. The car of the husband of my sister.

G. *Add a question word at the beginning and a preposition at the end of these sentences:*

E.g. *Who* is this present *for*?

1. . . . is she laughing . . .?
2. . . . are you going . . .?
3. . . . were you talking . . .?
4. . . . are you writing . . .?
5. . . . did you get . . .?
6. . . . station did they start . . .?
7. . . . are they waiting . . .?
8. . . . pen did you write . . .?
9. . . . are you staying . . .?

H. *Put the adverbs into the right place in these sentences:*

1. They go to a dance on New Year's Eve (*always*).
2. We met him in Edinburgh (*yesterday*).
3. The Browns go abroad for their holidays (*often*).
4. I go to church on Sunday, but I go during the week (*always, seldom*).
5. I read in bed before going to sleep (*usually*).
6. I have finished my lunch (*just*).
7. He was singing until we stopped him (*loudly*).
8. They left because they had to catch a bus (*early*).
9. He visits London but he does not come to see us (*often, usually*).

I. *Use short answers to disagree with the following:*

1. You don't have to go home yet.
2. Susan talks too much.
3. He went to Edinburgh last week.
4. I shall have to walk home.
5. There are plenty of cakes for tea.
6. You do love him, don't you?
7. She hasn't eaten all the chocolates, has she?
8. You're all working very hard, I know.
9. They must go home now.

J. *Put the verbs into the correct tense:*

Mrs Brown (*sit*) with her husband (*watch*) the dancers and (*think*) about the year that (*come*) to an end. She (*think*) too about all the other years that (*pass*) since she (*marry*). Before she (*marry*) John Brown, she (*live*) in the country. At first she and John (*live*) in London. After a time they (*move*) to Bishopton where they (*live*) now for ten years. Mrs Brown (*think*) too of the future. Soon Susan (*get married*) and David (*go*) off to the University. Then she and John (*not need*) a big house. Perhaps they (*sell*) this one and (*build*) a small one near London. No one (*know*) what (*happen*) in the future.

K. *Put the verbs in these sentences into the passive:*

1. Did anyone ever teach you English?
2. They refused his offer of help.
3. The heavy rain broke many flowers.
4. They left the children at home in bed.
5. Someone told him he could not take the examination.
6. They gave the work people at the factory a week's holiday.
7. Someone will tell her which bus to catch.
8. Many people invited us to their houses while we were in France.
9. They were building many new houses very quickly until they had used up all the empty land in town.
10. Someone wrote this book many centuries ago.

L. *Add relative pronouns where needed. Remember that, especially in spoken English, we leave out the relative when we can.*

1. The man . . . lives next door is a friend of ours.
2. Foreigners . . . come to London usually want to see Westminster Abbey.
3. The house . . . we saw yesterday is for sale.
4. The house . . . roof was on fire belongs to Mr Jones.
5. The clothes . . . she wears are always very smart.
6. The girl . . . I had the pen from is over there.
7. The man . . . drove us to the station said we should miss the train.
8. The train . . . we came in from London was late.
9. The handbag . . . I use every day is an old one.
10. The people . . . we invited to dinner can't come.

M. *Use each of these phrases in a sentence:*

quite an evening; just the thing; those were the days; a good many people; kind at heart; ready for anything; it can't be helped.

N. *Put* make *or* do *into these sentences:*

1. Mrs Brown . . . some cakes for tea.
2. Mrs Morton . . . her children change their shoes when they come home from school.
3. Will this dress . . . for the party, or shall I . . . a new one?
4. She has . . . the beds and . . . all her housework.
5. You . . . me laugh when you . . . that.
6. If you . . . your homework too quickly you'll . . . mistakes.
7. You should . . . up your mind to . . . away with all those tall trees in your garden.
8. I have . . . the bedrooms and . . . a nice fire in the sitting-room.
9. We have . . . all we can, but we can't . . . up for lost time.
10. I can't . . . my work while you're . . . all that noise.

O. *Add a time-clause to these sentences:*

1. Tom took a photograph of Susan . . .
2. . . . David told his father what he had seen.
3. Susan looked very pretty . . .
4. We have seen a lot of interesting places . . .
5. The road to Epsom is very crowded . . .
6. . . . Tom bought Susan a diamond ring.
7. . . . the members vote for or against what has been suggested.
8. . . . they caught the boat-train to London.
9. . . . the crowd cheered loudly.
10. . . . they went to bed, tired but happy.

P. *Write a composition about New Year's Day or some other important holiday in your own country.*

LIST OF SENTENCE PATTERNS

LIST OF IRREGULAR VERBS

This list includes all the Irregular Verbs introduced in Books One and Two of the Course. Special Verbs are marked thus*

Present	Past	Past Participle
become	became	become
begin	began	begun
blow	blew	blown
break	broke	broken
bring	brought	brought
buy	bought	bought
*can	could	
catch	caught	caught
choose	chose	chosen
come	came	come
cost	cost	cost
cut	cut	cut
dig	dug	dug
*do	did	done
draw	drew	drawn
drink	drank	drunk
drive	drove	driven
eat	ate	eaten
fall	fell	fallen
feed	fed	fed
feel	felt	felt
fight	fought	fought
find	found	found
fly	flew	flown
forget	forgot	forgotten

Present	Past	Past Participle
forgive	forgave	forgiven
freeze	froze	frozen
get	got	got
give	gave	given
go	went	gone
grow	grew	grown
hang	hung	hung
*have	had	had
hear	heard	heard
hide	hid	hidden
hit	hit	hit
hold	held	held
hurt	hurt	hurt
*is	was	been
keep	kept	kept
know	knew	known
lay	laid	laid
leave	left	left
lend	lent	lent
let	let	let
lie	lay	lain
lose	lost	lost
make	made	made
*may	might	
meet	met	met
*must		
*ought		
pay	paid	paid
put	put	put
read (*ri:d*)	read (*red*)	read (*red*)

Present	Past	Past Participle
ride	rode	ridden
ring	rang	rung
run	ran	run
say	said	said
see	saw	seen
sell	sold	sold
send	sent	sent
*shall	should	
shine	shone	shone
show	showed	shown
shut	shut	shut
sing	sang	sung
sit	sat	sat
sleep	slept	slept
speak	spoke	spoken
spend	spent	spent
spin	spun	spun
spread	spread	spread
stand	stood	stood
strike	struck	struck (stricken)
sweep	swept	swept
swim	swam	swum
take	took	taken
tear	tore	torn
tell	told	told
think	thought	thought
throw	threw	thrown
understand	understood	understood
wake	woke	woken
wear	wore	worn
*will	would	
win	won	won
write	wrote	written

INDEX TO THE EXERCISES

WORD LIST

The numbers refer to the pages on which
words first appear

crime (kraim), 107
  criminal ('kriminl), 206
cry (krai), 170
cushion ('kuʃn), 13
customs ('kʌstəmz), 204

dance (daːns)
  noun, 106; *verb*, 130
dangerous ('deindʒərəs), 112
dare (deə), 122
daresay (deə'sei), 121
date (deit), 171
dead (ded), 23
debate (di'beit), 185
deceit (də'siːt), 74
decide (di'said), 10
deck (dek), 207
degree (di'griː), 189
delightful (di'laitfəl), 188
department (di'paːtmənt), 120
depend (di'pend), 189
determine (di'təːmin), 106
diamond ('daiəmənd), 169
dictionary ('dikʃənri), 205
difference ('difrəns), 38
difficult ('difiklt), 114
  difficulty ('difiklti), 167
dine (dain), 138
director (di'rektə), 153
disappear (disə'piə), 204
distance ('distəns), 49
divide (di'vaid), 120
doctor ('doktə), 21
drama ('draːmə), 76
draw (droː), 222
dream (driːm), 221
duck (dʌk), 236

due (djuː), 207
dull (dʌl), 78
dust (dʌst), 10
duty ('djuːti), 242

ear (iə), 109
earn (eːn), 22
  earnings ('əːniŋz), 22
easily ('iːzili), 120
Easter ('iːstə), 184
eighteenth ('ei'tiːnθ), 134
either ('aiðə), 12
enclose (iŋ'klouz), 135
engaged (iŋ'geidʒd), 168
engine ('endʒin), 61
  engineer ('endʒi'niə), 60
  engineering ('endʒi'niəriŋ),
    60
enjoyable (ən'dʒoiəbl), 121
enter ('entə), 186
entertain ('entə'tein), 237
entrance ('entrns), 47
especially (is'peʃli), 107
even ('iːvn), 12
event (i'vent), 76
excellent ('eksələnt), 138
exciting (iks'aitiŋ), 49
expect (iks'pekt), 14
experience (iks'piəriəns), 170
explain (iks'plein), 133
extra ('ekstrə), 119
eye (ai), 109

face-powder ('feispaudə), 34
facing ('feisiŋ), 186
fact (fakt), 92
fair (feə), 155

faithfully ('feiθfəli), 135
famous ('feiməs), 107
fancy ('fansi), 253
farther ('faːðə), 234
fashionable ('faʃnəbl), 121
fault (foːlt), 109
feel (fiːl), 21
festival ('festəvəl), 76
fetch (fetʃ), 13
fiancé ('fiːaːnsei), 233
fight (fait), 207
fill (fil), 34
film (film), 34
finger ('fiŋgə), 169
firm (fəim), 135
fisherman ('fiʃəmən), 138
fit (fit), 61
fix (fiks), 64
flat (flat), 220
fly (flai), 78
fog (fog), 219
follow ('folou), 48
fond (fond), 118
foreign ('forin), 107
   foreigner ('forinə), 206
forget (fə'get), 13
forgive (fə'giv), 92
formal ('foːml), 236
frame (freim), 62
free (friː), 49
freeze (friːz), 207
friendly ('frendli), 92
fun (fʌn), 138
furniture ('fəːnitʃə), 10

gaiety ('geiiti), 236
gallery ('galəri), 185

gallon ('galən), 13
gather ('gaðə), 222
gentle ('dʒentl), 221
glasses ('glaːsiz), 22
goods (gudz), 120
great (greit), 22
grumble ('grʌmbl), 122
guide (gaid), 62
gun (gʌn), 206

hairdresser ('heədresə), 120
half-way ('haːf'wei), 203
hall (hoːl), 89
handle ('handl), 91
harbour ('haːbə), 204
hardly ('haːdli), 138
hate (heit), 159
haunt (hoːnt), 244
haystack ('heistak), 226
headache ('hedeik), 21
health (helθ), 22
heart (haːt), 206
hedge (hedʒ), 74
heel (hiːl), 62
heir (eə), 186
helper ('helpə), 15
herself (həː'self), 34
hide (haid), 136
high (hai), 35
himself (him'self), 35
historical (his'torikl), 107
home-made ('houm'meid), 91
honest ('onist), 170
hooray (hu'rei), 158
horse (hoːs), 154
   horseback ('hoːsbak), 68
hospital ('hospitl), 22

host (houst), 237
  hostess ('houstes), 237
hotel (hou'tel, ou'tel), 75
huge (hjuːdʒ), 155
hunt (hʌnt), 154

ice (ais), 112
idea (ai'diə), 49
impossible (im'posibl), 112
inch (intʃ), 63
indeed (in'diːd), 109
information (infə'meiʃn), 137
innings ('ininz), 221
introduce ('intrə'djuːs), 237
island ('ailənd), 206
isles (ailz), 78
itself (it'self), 162

jeweller ('dʒuələ), 169
job (dʒob), 92
join (dʒoin), 204
jolly ('dʒoli), 224
journey ('dʒəːni), 75
juice (dʒuːs), 121

key (kiː), 75
kick (kik), 244
killed (kild), 207
kind (kaind), 170
  kindly ('kaindli), 71
kiss (kis), 170
knee (niː), 207

lake (leik), 78
land (verb) (land), 204
language ('laŋgwidʒ), 47
last (verb) (laːst), 13
lately ('leitli), 119

law (loː), 185
lay (lei), 108
lazy ('leizi), 160
leaf, leaves (liːf, liːvz), 197
learner ('ləːnə), 15
least (liːst), 60
leather ('leðə), 120
lend (lend), 122
length (leŋkθ), 62
less (les), 81
library ('laibrəri), 49
lie (lai), 23
life (laif), 48
lift (noun) (lift), 75
lighter ('laitə), 218
lighthouse ('laithaus), 206
Limited (Ltd) ('limitid), 135
line (lain), 155
lip-stick ('lipstik), 34
listener ('lisnə), 15
lively ('laivli), 236
local ('loukəl), 205
lonely ('lounli), 49
lorry ('lori), 20
low (lou), 60
luck (lʌk), 253
  lucky ('lʌki), 121
luggage-rack ('lʌgidʒrak), 204
lump (lʌmp), 91

machine (mə'ʃiːn), 62
  machinery (mə'ʃiːnəri), 187
magazine (magə'ziːn), 131
maid (meid), 76
main (mein), 107
make-up ('meikʌp), 34
manage ('manidʒ), 35

petrol ('petrl), 208
photograph ('foutəgraɪf), 244
  photography (fə'togrəfi), 109
pin (pin), 260
pity ('piti), 97
plan (plan)
  noun, 91; *verb*, 208
plane (plein), 204
plant (plaɪnt),
  verb, 79; *noun*, 244
poet ('pouit), 207
  poetry ('pouətri), 108
politics ('politiks), 189
polish ('poliʃ), 244
poor (poɪ, puə), 138
popular ('popjulə), 154
possible ('posibl), 10
practice ('praktis), 205
prefer (pri'fəɪ), 91
preparation ('prepə'reiʃn), 220
presently ('prezəntli), 237
previous ('priɪviəs), 107
price (prais), 34
prize (praiz), 253
produce (*verb*) (prə'djuɪs), 187
profession (prə'feʃn), 189
progress ('prougres), 168
pronounce (prə'nauns), 91
proud (praud), 91
purple ('pəɪpl), 34
push (puʃ), 155

quarrel ('kworl), 137
quart (kwoɪt), 13
quay (kiɪ), 204
quick (kwik), 120
quite (kwait), 50

race (reis), 154
  race-course ('reiskoɪs), 154
rail (reil), 155
railway ('reilwei), 60
raise (reiz), 170
rather ('raɪðə), 23
razor ('reizə), 34
  razor-blade ('reizəbleid), 35
reader ('riɪdə), 15
receive (ri'siɪv), 137
recommend ('rekə'mend), 138
record-player ('rekoɪd pleiə),
  237
refuse (ri'fjuɪz), 93
relation (ri'leiʃn), 136
remark (ri'maɪk), 236
remind (ri'maind), 138
require (ri'kwaiə), 51
reserved (ri'zəɪvd), 204
result (ri'zʌlt), 50
retire (ri'taiə), 244
rich (ritʃ), 154
rider ('raidə), 15
ring (riŋ), 169
robes (roubz), 187
rock (rok), 76
row (rou), 185
rubber ('rʌbə), 61
rule (ruɪl), 167
run (*noun*) (rʌn), 221
runner ('rʌnə), 15
rushing ('rʌʃiŋ), 139

sack (sak), 185
saddle ('sadl), 61
safe (seif), 156
  safety ('seifti), 155

wish (wiʃ)
   noun, 50; *verb*, 135
wonder ('wʌndə), 206
   wonderful ('wʌndəfl), 78
wooden ('wudn), 188
workshop ('wəɪkʃop), 62
world (wəɪld), 61
worry ('wʌri), 21
worse (wəɪs), 21
   worst (wəɪst), 34

would (wud), 39
wrap (rap), 33
wrist (rist), 93
writer ('raitə), 15
   writing-paper ('raitiŋ
   peipə), 34

yard (jaɪd), 62
yourself, yourselves (joɪ'self,
   joɪ'selvz), 35

NAMES OF PLACES

(All these begin with capital letters)

Aberdeen ('abə'diɪn)
America (ə'merikə)
   American (ə'merikən)
Arthur's Seat ('aɪθəz 'siɪt)
Australia (os'treiljə)
   Australian (os'treiljən)
Bakerloo Line ('beikə'luɪ lain)
Battersea Power Station
   ('batəsiɪ 'pauə steiʃn)
British Commonwealth, The
   'britiʃ 'komənwelθ, ðə)
Calais ('kalei)
Derby ('daɪbi)
District Line ('distrikt lain)
Dover ('douvə)
English Channel ('ingliʃ
   'tʃanl)
Epsom Downs ('epsəm
   'daunz)
France (fraɪns)

French (frentʃ)
   Frenchman ('frentʃmən)
Germany ('dʒəɪməni)
   German ('dʒəɪmən)
Haymarket ('heimaɪkit)
Highlands, The ('hailəndz, ðə)
Holyroodhouse ('holiruɪd'haus)
House of Commons ('haus
   əv 'komənz)
House of Lords ('haus əv
   'loɪdz)
India ('indiə)
   Indian ('indiən)
Italy ('itəli)
   Italian (i'taljən)
Kent (kent)
King's Cross Station ('kiŋz
   'kros 'steiʃn)
Lake District ('leik distrikt)
Lincoln ('linkən)

London Airport ('lʌndən 'eəpoɪt)

Lord's Cricket Ground (loɪdz 'krikit graund)

Merton College ('məɪtən 'kolidʒ)

Newmarket ('njuɪmaɪkit)

New Zealand (njuɪ 'ziɪlənd)
  New Zealander (njuɪ 'ziɪləndə)

Nottingham ('notiŋəm)

The Oval (Cricket Ground) (θi 'ouvl)

Pakistan (pakis'taɪn)
  Pakistani (pakis'taɪni)

Princes Street ('prinsiz striɪt)

Queen's College ('kwiɪnz 'kolidʒ)

Queen's Hotel ('kwiɪnz hou'tel)

Regent Street ('riɪdʒənt striɪt)

Royal Albert Hall ('roiəl 'albət 'hoɪl)

St Giles' Cathedral (snt 'dʒailz kə'θiɪdrl)

St Stephen's Hall (snt 'stiɪvnz hoɪl)

Sheffield ('ʃefiɪld)

South Africa (sauθ 'afrikə)
  South African (sauθ 'afrikən)

Spain (spein)
  Spanish ('spaniʃ)
  Spaniard ('spanjəd)

Stratford-on-Avon ('stratfəd on 'eivn)

Victoria Tower (vik'toɪriə 'tauə)

Waverley Station ('weivəli 'steiʃn)

Western Isles ('westən 'ailz)

West Indies ('west 'indiz)
  West Indian ('west 'indiən)

Westminster Hall ('westminstə 'hoɪl)

BOYS' NAMES

Arthur ('aɪθə)

Donald ('donəld)

Douglas ('dʌgləs)

Geoffrey ('dʒefri)

Gordon ('goɪdn)

Henry (Harry) ('henri, 'hari)

Ian ('iən)

Norman ('noɪmən)

Peter ('piɪtə)

Philip ('filip)

Stanley ('stanli)

Stephen ('stiɪvn)

William (Bill) ('wiljəm, bil)

GIRLS' NAMES

Anne (an)
Betty ('beti)
Dorothy ('dorəθi)
Freda ('friːdə)

Helen ('helin)
Jean (dʒiːn)
Maud (moːd)
Pamela ('pamələ)

FAMILY NAMES

Barton ('baːtn)
Benson ('bensn)
Bentley ('bentli)
Bradman ('bradmən)
Carter ('kaːtə)
Clarke (klaːk)
Cuthbert ('kʌθbət)
Dawson ('doːsn)
Dixon ('diksn)
Gamage ('gamidʒ)
Harris ('haris)
Harrison ('harisn)

Harrods ('harədz)
Higgins ('higinz)
Hobbs (hobz)
Jackson ('dʒaksn)
Macdonald (mak'donld)
Miller ('milə)
Nokes (nouks)
Richards ('ritʃədz)
Rowlands ('rouləndz)
Selfridge ('selfridʒ)
Shakespeare ('ʃeikspiə)
Turner ('təːnə)

GRAMMATICAL TERMS

ability (ə'biliti)
active ('aktiv)
affirmative (ə'fəɪmətiv)
agent ('eidʒnt)
anomalous (ə'nomələs)
appear (ə'piə)
article ('aɪtikl)
attempt (ə'tempt)
attention (ə'tenʃn)
auxiliary (ɔɪg'ziljəri)

case (keis)
challenge ('tʃalindʒ)
collective (kə'lektiv)
comma ('komə)
compound ('kompaund)
concerned (kən'səɪnd)
concession (kən'seʃn)
conditional (kən'diʃnəl)
conjunction (kən'dʒʌŋkʃn)
control (kən'troul)
correct (kə'rekt)
countable ('kauntəbl)
customary ('kʌstəm(ə)ri)

definite ('definət, 'definit)
description (dis'kripʃn)
desire (di'zaiə)
direct (di'rekt)
    indirect ('indi'rekt)

emphasise ('emfəsaiz)
    emphatic (im'fatik)
exist (ig'zist)
exclamation (eksklə'meiʃn)
express (iks'pres)
    expression (iks'preʃn)

finite ('fainait)
form (fɔɪm)
frequency ('friɪkwənsi)

general ('dʒenrəl)

idiomatic (idiə'matik)
imaginary (i'madʒinri)
impersonal (im'pəɪsənl)
indefinite (in'definət,
    in'definit)
indirect (indai'rekt)
intensive (in'tensiv)
interrogative ('intə'rogətiv)
inversion (in'vəɪʃn)

limit ('limit)

manner ('manə)
materials (mə'tiəriəlz)
mean (miɪn)
meaning ('miɪniŋ)

necessary ('nesisri)
notice ('noutis)

obligation (ˈobliˈgeiʃn)
  obligatory (oˈbligətri)
obtain (əbˈtein)
ordinary (ˈoːdinri)

paragraph (ˈparəgraːf)
particular (pəˈtikjulə)
passive (ˈpasiv)
perform (pəˈfoːm)
permission (pəˈmiʃn)
phrasal (ˈfreizl)
possibility (posiˈbiliti)
predicate (ˈpredikət)
probable (ˈprobəbl)
  probably (ˈprobəbli)

quantity (ˈkwontiti)

reason (ˈriːzən)
reflexive (riˈfleksiv)
repetition (ˈrepəˈtiʃn)
reported (riˈpoːtid)
request (riˈkwest)
require (riˈkwaiə)
result (riˈzʌlt)

shorten (ˈʃoːtn)
speech (spiːtʃ)
state (steit)
statement (ˈsteitmənt)
sufficient (səˈfiʃnt)

translate (ˈtransˈleit)

uncountable (ʌnˈkauntəbl)